LESSONS LEARNED IN GLOBAL ENVIRONMENTAL GOVERNANCE

Peter H. Sand

WORLD RESOURCES INSTITUTE

June 1990

Kathleen Courrier
Publications Director

Brooks Clapp
Marketing Manager

Hyacinth Billings
Production Manager

United Nations/T. Chen
Cover Photo

Each World Resources Institute Report represents a timely, scientific treatment of a subject of public concern. WRI takes responsibility for choosing the study topics and guaranteeing its authors and researchers freedom of inquiry. It also solicits and responds to the guidance of advisory panels and expert reviewers. Unless otherwise stated, however, all the interpretation and findings set forth in WRI publications are those of the authors.

Contents

Foreword

Several trends are acting together to push environmental concerns toward the front and center of the international stage. More and more, pollution is transboundary and even global in scope, threatening to damage the stratospheric ozone shield and alter climate and sea levels worldwide. Pressures on shared resources, such as river basins and coastal fisheries, are mounting. Massive deforestation by one region can alter another's hydrological cycle and the world's carbon cycle, even as it diminishes the global stock of biological resources. Resource deterioration in many nations is so severe that it registers in neighboring countries—when, for instance, ecological refugees flee across borders. And in the growing global marketplace, domestic environmental policies that affect business, industry, and agriculture need to be harmonized at the international level. Economic integration is also forcing environmental integration.

It is not just that there are more environmental problems so large that they can be intelligently dealt with only at the international level; it is also that the line between national and international environmental problems is fast disappearing. Nitrogen oxide emissions, for example, must be regulated locally because of ground-level ozone formation, regionally because of acid rain, and globally because ground-level ozone is a heat-trapping "greenhouse" gas.

In this instance, domestic and global environmental concerns push in the same direction, but in others they operate at cross purposes. Consider, for example, the case of alternative fuels. A car burning methanol made from coal emits perhaps twice as much carbon dioxide per mile as one burning gasoline does. So switching from gasoline to methanol might improve local and regional air quality—at the cost of increasing the global warming risk.

Environmental diplomacy is the logical outgrowth of the desire to protect one's own national environment, to minimize environment-related conflicts with other countries, and to realize mutual benefits, including economic progress and the protection of humankind's common natural heritage. As such, it is not entirely new. The register of international environmental conventions and protocols has grown steadily in this century; the main multilateral treaties today number more than 100, many of them aimed at protecting wildlife and the marine environment. What is new is the prospect that environmental issues will move from a secondary to a primary international concern and increasingly crowd the diplomatic agendas of nations. This diplomacy will increasingly affect domestic environmental policy.

No one knows exactly what the challenge of "internationalization" will ultimately require. Major policy and institutional innovations will clearly be needed, but the bottom line is that national environmental policy will more and more be set in concert with other nations.

And, outside of government, international business codes of conduct and other transnational norms will become far more common.

How can international environmental standard-setting and implementation practices be upgraded? What can be learned from our experience to date, which is more extensive than most imagine? How can we beat the lowest-common-denominator and slowest-boat syndromes that plague treaty-making? What alternatives to litigation can settle environmental disputes between nations? It is to these important questions that Peter H. Sand, a seasoned expert in international law and a pioneer in this new field, turns in this report.

Drawing on past environmental diplomacy to illuminate his points, Dr. Sand examines ways to tune up existing institutional machinery to deal with the tough decisions that lie ahead. He uses the 1973 Washington *Convention on International Trade in Endangered Species of Wild Flora and Fauna,* for instance, as an example of how "selective incentives" broaden the appeal of conservation agreements, in this case by offering economic benefits to otherwise reluctant parties. He points to the West German "blue angel" environmental label, introduced in 1978, to illustrate how models spread—in this case to Canada, Japan, and Scandinavia, all of which developed such labels in 1989. And he discusses how the 1987 *Montreal Protocol on Substances That Deplete the Ozone Layer* ensures the flexibility increasingly needed to keep international regimes attuned to the latest scientific evidence and to changing environmental and economic conditions.

Peter H. Sand is senior environmental affairs officer with the United Nations Economic Commission for Europe in Geneva. A German citizen and international lawyer, he has been involved in environmental management, diplomatic negotiations, and treaty-making for the past twenty years. Before taking the UN/ECE post, Dr. Sand served as chief of the environmental law unit at the United Nations Environment Programme, as assistant director general of the International Union for Conservation of Nature and Natural Resources (IUCN), and as senior legal officer with the United Nations Food and Agriculture Organization.

This study complements WRI's ongoing research on what roles global and regional institutions can play in tackling today's environmental agenda and how they advance and support the application of legal frameworks to deal with environmental problems.

WRI would like to express its great appreciation to the John D. and Catherine T. MacArthur Foundation, The John Merck Fund, and the Compton Foundation, Inc., which have provided financial support for WRI's efforts in this area.

James Gustave Speth
President
World Resources Institute

Introduction: A Memory Unfrozen

For two reasons, our generation will bear a heavier responsibility for the future of planet Earth than any generation before it has. First, we know better—having gained access to an unprecedented wealth of new scientific information and a vastly improved capacity for analysis and prediction. Second, we can do better—having accumulated enough experience, technological and institutional, to take the necessary international action.

The first point needs little elaboration. The ongoing research of a team of French and Russian palaeo-glaciologists, which has proven the link between global warming and "greenhouse gases" in our atmosphere, is but one of many examples of the expanding knowledge base.[1] This breakthrough analysis was carried out on a 2000-metre-deep ice core excavated by the Soviet Antarctic Expeditions in Vostok, East Antarctica. Each successive layer of ice in the Vostok core contains myriad air bubbles trapped and hermetically sealed—in the case of the bottom-most layers, for up to 160,000 years. Crushing the bubbles in laboratories in Grenoble and Saclay (France), scientists were able to identify their exact chemical composition by gas chromatography and to determine their age by calculating the rate of ice sedimentation.

The net outcome of this analysis—which involved technology and computer calculations more sophisticated than any used even a few years ago—was a continuous historical record not only of the Earth's atmospheric conditions but also of the corresponding temperature changes on the surface of Antarctica. *(See Figure 1).* The obvious next step was to compare this priceless new data base with other available information, including similar ice cores from Siple Station in Western Antarctica and from Greenland, maritime data from the Indian Ocean region, and more recent global monitoring data on atmospheric chemistry—for example, the continuous carbon dioxide measurements from the Mauna Loa station in Hawaii, which began in 1958. *(See Figure 2).* What experts found was that the most recent ice-core data for carbon dioxide (CO_2) in Antarctic air matched contemporary Mauna Loa measurements of atmospheric CO_2: both show a clear and steep upward trend. They also show a consistent correlation between the rise and fall in carbon dioxide, methane (the second major "greenhouse gas"), and global temperature, although we do not know the details of cause and effect.

The significant message here is not only the new empirical evidence contributing to our understanding of the greenhouse effect. Even more striking is the degree of international scientific cooperation through which this evidence has been produced. Reconsider the sequence: the Vostok ice core was drilled and extracted by Soviet Antarctic expeditions as part of the scientific programs authorized under the Antarctic Treaty; under a French-Russian

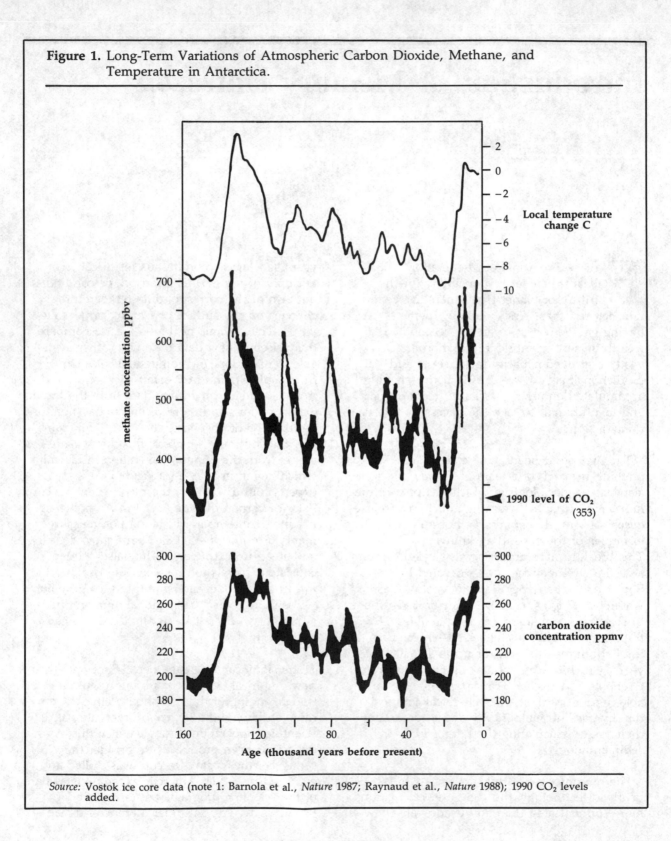

Figure 1. Long-Term Variations of Atmospheric Carbon Dioxide, Methane, and Temperature in Antarctica.

Local temperature change C

700

methane concentration ppbv

600

500

400

◀ 1990 level of CO_2 (353)

300

280

260

240

220

200

180

carbon dioxide concentration ppmv

160   120   80   40   0

Age (thousand years before present)

Source: Vostok ice core data (note 1: Barnola et al., *Nature* 1987; Raynaud et al., *Nature* 1988); 1990 CO_2 levels added.

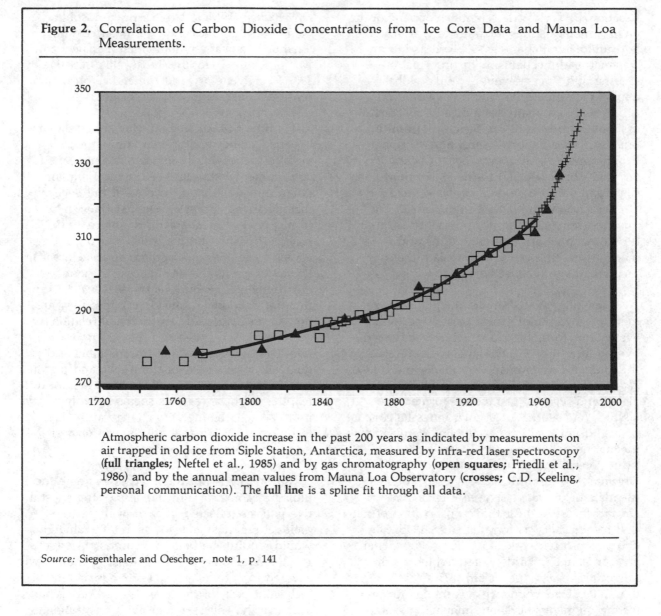

Figure 2. Correlation of Carbon Dioxide Concentrations from Ice Core Data and Mauna Loa Measurements.

Atmospheric carbon dioxide increase in the past 200 years as indicated by measurements on air trapped in old ice from Siple Station, Antarctica, measured by infra-red laser spectroscopy (**full triangles;** Neftel et al., 1985) and by gas chromatography (**open squares;** Friedli et al., 1986) and by the annual mean values from Mauna Loa Observatory (**crosses;** C.D. Keeling, personal communication). The **full line** is a spline fit through all data.

Source: Siegenthaler and Oeschger, note 1, p. 141

agreement, the whole sample was analyzed in laboratories in France; the data were then compared with other ice-core data obtained by Swiss glaciologists at an Australian Antarctic station and with atmospheric chemistry data from an American monitoring station in Hawaii; and the results were eventually reviewed and published in a British science magazine.

The sequence doesn't end here either: The new Antarctic evidence is now before the *Intergovernmental Panel on Climate Change* (IPCC) set up in 1988 by the World Meteorological Organization (WMO) and the United Nations Environment Programme (UNEP). The IPCC will use the data in its report to the second World Climate Conference in Geneva in November 1990, as a basis for specific recommendations for action by governments.

Clearly, the international machinery for environmental assessment is well established and functional. Worldwide scientific cooperation on environmental issues includes formal bilateral and multilateral channels, as well as informal transnational mechanisms for information-sharing and "peer review." While global demand for environmental knowledge continues to grow, many examples of successful assessment programs are at hand—from the ongoing "International Geosphere-Biosphere Programme"[2] of the *International Council of Scientific Unions* (ICSU) to the 1987 report of the *World Commission on Environment and Development* (Brundtland Commission).[3] The question remains: how well established and how functional are the institutions and mechanisms that can now translate these assessments into collective action?

As for international environmental management or governance,[4] most current performance evaluations focus on the structure established by and after the 1972 Stockholm Conference on the Human Environment,[5] primarily the *United Nations Environment Programme* (UNEP) and global and regional institutions formed after UNEP. Yet, international environmental cooperation did not begin at Stockholm. Conventions for marine pollution control were drafted twenty years earlier by the *International Maritime Organization* (then IMCO). The constitutional mandate of the U.N. *Food and Agriculture Organization* (FAO) for the "conservation of natural resources" was formulated in 1945. Standards to protect workers against occupational environmental hazards were adopted by the *International Labour Organization* (ILO) as early as the 1920s. Transboundary agreements for protecting migratory birds and managing shared water resources date to well before World War I, as do international arrangements by 19th-century precursors of the *World Meteorological Organization* (WMO) for sharing atmospheric data. And the first serious, if unsuccessful, attempt at global environmental management was probably Theodore Roosevelt's initiative in 1909 to convene a world conference on natural resource conservation at The Hague.

It is time to take stock of this accumulated experience and institutional know-how, with a view to identifying innovative mechanisms for environmental standard-setting and implementation directly related to some of the decision-making ahead. Political scientists have referred to this type of mechanisms as international *regimes* (that is, "norms, rules and procedures agreed to in order to regulate an issue-area").[6] It may be preferable in this case to define environmental regimes as *transnational* rather than international,[7] considering that they are not confined to intergovernmental relations between nation-states and that many are hybrids—partaking of the international and domestic legal order, of the public and private law sector. In fact, one of the most significant features of these regimes seems to be their ability to switch channels, to change and adapt techniques when needed in light of experience—in short, to innovate.

This survey is not intended to evaluate the ultimate ecological effectiveness of the substantive policies reflected in each of these transnational regimes. Indeed, such an evaluation would require the benefit of hindsight over a much longer timespan than most of them have covered to date. (Twenty years equals ten inches, at best, of the Vostok ice core.) What is available, however, is a growing institutional memory of managerial methods for coping with some typical obstacles to effective international environmental governance.

I. Innovations in Standard-Setting

Traditionally, international standards have been set through treaties. An *ad hoc* diplomatic conference negotiates and adopts a treaty, which then has to undergo national ratification (usually by parliaments) to become legally binding. International environmental law-making poses no exception to this rule: typically, therefore, most recent proposals for international action on global warming envisage a convention on climate change[8] or on a "law of the atmosphere,"[9] along the lines of the United Nations' 1982 Montego Bay *Convention on the Law of the Sea.*[10]

As distinct from national environmental legislation, however, treaty rules laid down by conventional diplomatic "ad-hocracy"[11] have two fundamental drawbacks:

Unlike decisions by a national legislature, internationally agreed-upon standards tend to reflect the lowest common denominator—the bottomline.

First, they are based on the consensus or unanimity of all participants since no sovereign state is obliged to sign or ratify any treaty. Unlike decisions by a national legislature, which normally result in a median standard determined by majority vote that also binds the outvoted minority, internationally agreed-upon standards thus tend to reflect the lowest common denominator—the bottomline.

Second, parliamentary ratification takes time, so the effectiveness of international agreements is deliberately delayed. Unlike national laws—which can fix their own dates of application, even allowing for immediate applicability or amendment—multilateral treaties can be brought into force, or amended, only after a specified number of signatories ratifies them. The purpose, of course, is to ensure a measure of reciprocity and to avoid situations in which initial compliance by a few diligent parties creates disproportionate benefits to the "free-riders" remaining outside the treaty. Setting a threshold number, however, also delays implementation to the speed of the slowest boat in the convoy.

It has often been pointed out how antiquated and cumbersome this conventional process is.[12] Diplomatic treaty-making may be a useful way to formulate principles of behavior and a framework for intergovernmental relations. But are traditional treaty techniques suitable for effective environmental governance at the global or regional scale once international action must pass from declarations to operations? Environmental problems frequently involve unforeseeable changes of circumstances—sometimes under crisis conditions—in the face of continuous scientific-technological progress. Critical to successful international management, therefore, is a normative system's capacity to respond to frequent and rapid change. If the classical treaty—that "sadly overworked instrument"[13]—lacks this capacity, what are the alternatives?

While it is difficult to see how the traditional treaty process can be avoided altogether, there are ways to deal with some of its shortcomings.

While it is difficult to see how the traditional treaty process can be avoided altogether, there are ways to deal with some of its shortcomings. A few of such alternatives—in Mancur Olson's terms, "politically feasible ways to increase the incentives for collectively rational behavior"[14]—are sketched here in light of practical experience with transnational environmental standards.

Asymmetrical Standards: How to Beat the Bottomline Rule

Multilateral agreements based on the lowest common denominator are well documented. In international fishery regimes, for example, a "law of the least ambitious program" has been diagnosed by a Norwegian political scientist, Arild Underdal:

> "Where international management can be established only through agreement among all significant parties involved, and where such a regulation is considered only on its own merits, collective action will be limited to those measures acceptable to the least enthusiastic party."[15]

Significantly, though, Underdal goes on to note, a reluctant party can often be persuaded to modify its position through "arguments, side-payments, or various kinds of political pressure."

Even Underdal's catalogue of exceptions to the rule of the least ambitious program is far from exhaustive. As negotiating experience in the wider field of international environmental agreements shows, options for making ambitious programs or better-than-minimum standards attractive to parties include selective incentives, differential obligations, recourse to regional solidarity, and promotion of over-achievement by lead countries.

Selective Incentives. The concept of "selective incentives" is well established in economic group theory[16] as one motive for collective action. It simply means that certain fringe-benefits may persuade a party to participate in a program or standard that it would otherwise find unacceptable. The familiar parliamentary practice of coalition-building and majority-building by judicious distribution of special favors has obvious parallels in the negotiation of multilateral treaties.

A case in point is the 1987 *Montreal Protocol on Substances That Deplete the Ozone Layer.*[17] Under article 2(5), production increases by way of "transfers" were authorized between small-scale producers; by virtue of article 2(6), the USSR was granted "grandfather rights" for factories under construction until the end of 1990; in article 2(8), the member states of the European Community were authorized to aggregate their national consumption limits; in article 5, developing countries were allowed to postpone compliance by ten years; etc.

It is easy to criticize the Montreal text as a compromise full of loopholes built in to accommodate special interests.[18] But without these "rider" clauses, the agreement would either have lost some important signatories or jelled at a lower level of collective commitment. Paradoxically, loopholes can *upgrade* the overall standard of obligations in an agreement—raising them above the predictable common denominator.

In environmental treaty bargaining, the selective incentives commonly used are access to funding, access to resources, access to markets, and access to technology. Access to funding as an incentive to adhere to international conservation standards is perhaps best illustrated by the 1972 *Convention for the Protection of the World Cultural and Natural Heritage*[19]—which, with 111 member States, is the most widely accepted environmental treaty today. Under articles 13 and 19 of the convention, parties are eligible for financial assistance from the World Heritage Fund to support conservation measures for national sites included in a "world heritage list" if they maintain these sites at agreed standards of protection. The fund—administered by the *United Nations Educational, Scientific and Cultural Organization* (UNESCO)—now has an annual budget of $2.2 million financed by both mandatory and voluntary contributions and split about evenly between projects for cultural and natural heritage sites.[20]

In environmental treaty bargaining, the selective incentives commonly used are access to funding, access to resources, access to markets, and access to technology.

Access to the sustainable use of natural resources is an economic incentive for participating in many international regimes aimed at reconciling rational exploitation and conservation. Wide-ranging examples of this incentive include the annual catch quota established under numerous regional agreements for marine fishing and seal hunting,[21] and the worldwide 1946 *International Convention for the Regulation of Whaling*[22] (until the entry into force of the moratorium in 1986), and the 1980 Canberra *Convention on the Conservation of Antarctic Marine Living Resources*.[23] The acceptance of environmental restrictions in return for the prospect of sharing mineral resources is as much a part of the U.N. Law of the Sea Convention as of the 1988 Wellington *Convention on the Regulation of Antarctic Mineral Resource Activities*.[24] Similarly, access to the world market for wildlife and wildlife products, in return for observing agreed-upon conservation standards, has been recognized as an economic incentive for countries to join the 1973 Washington *Convention on International Trade in Endangered Species of Wild Fauna and Flora* (CITES),[25] which led to specific quota schemes for marketing "controlled" crocodile hides and (until 1989) ivory.[26]

A more recent addition to the catalogue of selective incentives in international regimes is access to technology. This was first and most prominently used as an incentive for participation in the 1968 *Treaty on the Non-proliferation of Nuclear Weapons*.[27] While early environmental treaties (such as the UNEP-sponsored regional seas conventions and protocols since 1976) contain only general recommendations on technical assistance to developing countries,[28] specific provisions to facilitate technology transfer have appeared in recent agreements, from the 1985 *Vienna Convention for the Protection of the Ozone Layer*[29] to the 1989 *Basel Convention on the Control of Transboundary Movements of Hazardous Wastes and Their Disposal*.[30] In this context, the 1990 review of the Montreal Protocol will consider the establishment of an international trust fund for transferring technology and financial assistance to developing countries.[31] Clauses for the preferential acquisition of new environmental technology have become a major bargaining issue not only in North-South negotiations but also in East-West relations. For instance, a provision on "procedures to create more favorable conditions for the exchange of technology to reduce emissions of nitrogen oxides" was considered by East European countries (faced with Western export restrictions on strategic high technology) as one prerequisite for accepting the 1988 Sofia Protocol to the *Convention on Long-range Transboundary Air Pollution*.[32] An intergovernmental task force on technology exchange has since been set up under the auspices of the Executive Body for the Convention.[33]

Differential Obligations. Since selective incentives by definition lead to special treatment for selected parties, they skew an otherwise symmetrical system of reciprocal rights and obligations. Such manifest discrimination, particularly in the case of last-minute "add-ons," can seriously undermine the credibility of a multilateral agreement. Consequently, a more straightforward alternative is to start out with an asymmetrical regime that does not even pretend to treat states equally, and instead differentiates treaty obligations according to each party's special circumstances.

As an example, the European Community's *Directive on the Limitation of Emissions of Certain Pollutants into the Air from Large Combustion Plants*[34] of 24 November 1988 lays down a country-by-country timeplan, taking into account the particular economic and technological situation in each of the twelve member states. While Belgium, France, the Netherlands, and the Federal Republic of Germany are to reduce their sulphur dioxide emissions 70 percent by the year 2003, the target for Denmark was set at 67 percent, for Italy at 63 percent, and for Luxembourg and the United Kingdom at 60 percent; at the same time, Greece, Ireland, and Portugal were allowed to increase emissions temporarily.

Skewed as these obligations may seem, they resemble the differential assessment scales that have been developed for multilateral funding of numerous environmental agreements. Under the 1976 Bonn *Convention for the Protection of the Rhine Against Pollution by Chlorides*,[35] for instance, the four riparian countries—the Netherlands, the Federal Republic of Germany, France, and Switzerland—agreed to share abatement costs (currently estimated at a total of $136 million) in percentages of 34:30:30:6, respectively.

The various U.N. trust funds set up since 1977 to finance joint programs under the Mediterranean Convention (annual budget $3.8 million), the Endangered Species Convention ($1.6 million), the Transboundary Air Pollution Convention ($1 million), and the Ozone Layer Convention ($1 million with the Montreal Protocol) all use weighted contributions based on the global assessment scale laid down by the U.N. General Assembly. In this system, countries are rated according to a combination of economic, geographic, and demographic criteria. (The only political limit to this prorated scheme is a 25-percent "ceiling" for individual contributions, introduced in 1972 at U.S. insistence that no single party should be assessed at more than one quarter of the total budget.[36])

Differential scales enable even the smallest countries to participate on an equal footing without de-stabilizing a treaty's budget.

Differential scales enable even the smallest countries to participate on an equal footing without de-stabilizing a treaty's budget. Indeed, under the Vienna/Montreal ozone layer agreements, Singapore contributes $1500 annually but exercises the same membership rights as the United States, which pays $300,000.

Such skewing is carried one step farther by the "critical loads" approach now being developed in the context of the Transboundary Air Pollution Convention. As defined in the 1988 Sofia *Protocol Concerning the Control of Emissions of Nitrogen Oxides or Their Transboundary Fluxes*, critical load means "a quantitative estimate of the exposure to one or more pollutants below which significant harmful effects on specified sensitive elements of the environment do not occur according to present knowledge."[37] When this approach is translated into national abatement targets, it is bound to lead to differential obligations (equitable rather than equal) for each party. The basic logic resembles that behind the concept of ''safe minimum standards''[38] in natural resources management, which also aims at the equitable allocation of a common property resource without jeopardizing its long-term conservation for all users. Yet, the transition from ''egalitarian'' flat rates to highly individualized allocations also introduces a new level of complexity in environmental regimes—witness the amount of computer time now being spent on allocation models.[39]

Regionalization. Custom-built asymmetrical regimes are, of course, more easily achieved among regional groups of countries, where economic and other trade-offs can compensate for the asymmetries. Furthermore, if broadening the scope of an international regime means lowering its common denominator (with universal membership at the absolute bottomline), then the reverse should also be true: restricting membership should raise the standard, particularly where such restriction reflects an element of geographic or other affinity between members.[40]

Does international experience in environmental governance bear out this observation? Certainly, the degree of institutional cooperation accomplished under regional agreements for marine environment protection (*see Figure 3*)— such as the 1974 Helsinki and Paris Conventions for the Baltic and the North Sea[41] and the UNEP regional seas agreements starting with the 1976 Barcelona *Convention for the Protection of the Mediterranean Sea Against Pollution*[42]—has consistently been higher than under comparable global regimes, except possibly for ship-based pollution regulation by the International Maritime Organization (IMO).[43] At a time when the U.N. Law of the Sea Convention (with its chapter XII on global protection and preservation of the marine environment) has still not entered into force, more than 50 states are already legally bound by conventions and protocols concluded under U.N. environment programs for the Mediterranean, the Caribbean,

the West-Central African coast, the Red Sea, the Gulf, and the Southeast Pacific.[44] And while UNEP's own global guidelines on offshore mining (1982) and on land-based marine pollution (1985)[45] generated little more than lip-service from governments,[46] many countries did accept emission standards and specific regional commitments to prevent and abate marine pollution under the UNEP-sponsored Athens (1980) and Quito (1983) Protocols on pollution from land-based sources[47] and under the Kuwait (1989) Protocol on pollution from exploration and exploitation of the continental shelf.[48]

Far from offering a panacea for all transnational environmental problems, regional regulation may be manifestly unsuitable for some.

But if regionalization can raise the level of standards, it can also introduce further asymmetries or reinforce existing ones. Far from offering a panacea for all transnational environmental problems, regional regulation may be manifestly unsuitable for some. For instance, when the *Organisation for Economic Cooperation and Development* (OECD) in 1984 initiated a regional draft convention for transboundary shipments of hazardous wastes,[49] it was able to draw on a higher level of solidarity and consensus among its membership (limited to Western industrialized states) than would have been conceivable under a worldwide treaty. On the other hand, it soon became clear that the very prospect of tightened waste controls in the OECD region had an undesired spill-over effect, reorienting trade flows to countries outside the region that were unlikely to abide by OECD-imposed regulation.[50] The OECD member states eventually had to abandon their project in favor of a less ambitious but globally applicable regime under UNEP auspices, the

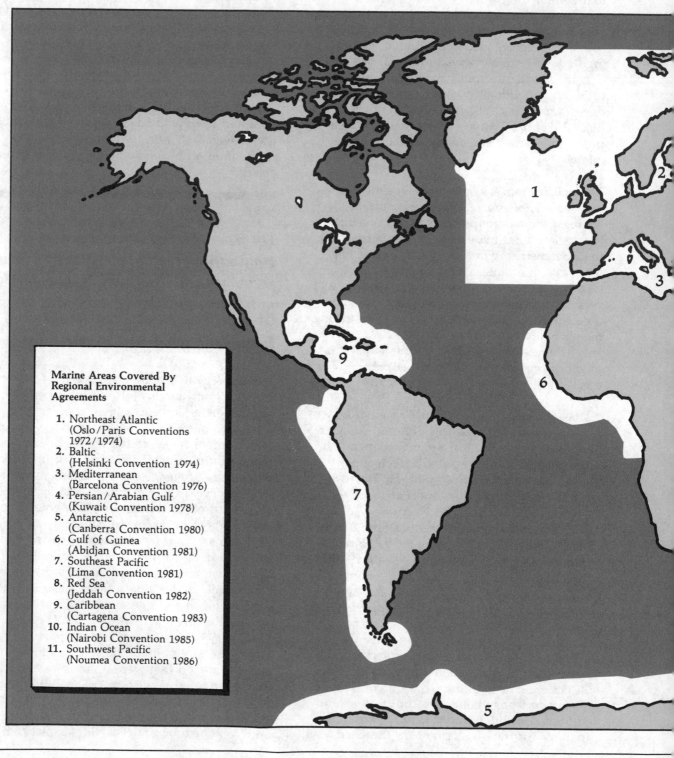

Figure 3. Map Showing Ocean Areas Covered by Regional Conventions for Marine Environment Protection.

Marine Areas Covered By Regional Environmental Agreements

1. Northeast Atlantic
(Oslo/Paris Conventions 1972/1974)
2. Baltic
(Helsinki Convention 1974)
3. Mediterranean
(Barcelona Convention 1976)
4. Persian/Arabian Gulf
(Kuwait Convention 1978)
5. Antarctic
(Canberra Convention 1980)
6. Gulf of Guinea
(Abidjan Convention 1981)
7. Southeast Pacific
(Lima Convention 1981)
8. Red Sea
(Jeddah Convention 1982)
9. Caribbean
(Cartagena Convention 1983)
10. Indian Ocean
(Nairobi Convention 1985)
11. Southwest Pacific
(Noumea Convention 1986)

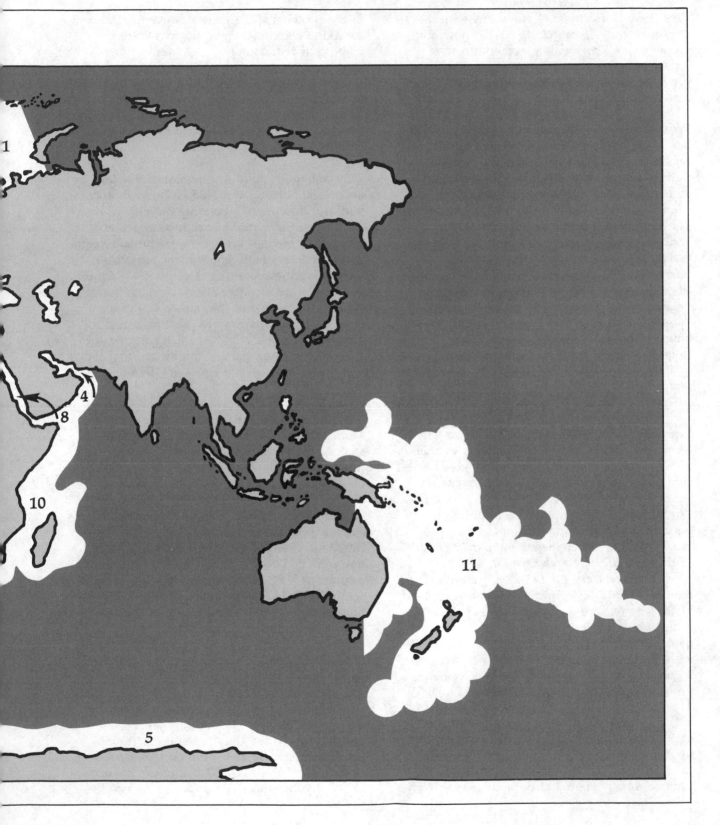

1989 Basel Convention.[51] However, with the *Organization of African Unity* (OAU) now drafting a separate regional agreement on the topic,[52] the waste trade issue will continue to provide trial-and-error lessons in transnational regime-building.

Promoting Over-Achievement. To be sure, the Basel Convention does not prevent additional regional action. Article 11 actually reserves the right of any party to enter into other arrangements that are "not less environmentally sound" than the agreed-upon global standards. The European Community has already announced its intention to implement the convention by tighter requirements,[53] as it previously did with such other treaties as the Council of Europe's 1968 Strasbourg *Agreement on the Restriction of the Use of Certain Detergents in Washing and Cleaning Products.*[54] (The Strasbourg Convention, which required detergents to be at least 80 percent "biodegradable," was upstaged by a 1973 EEC Detergents Directive requiring at least 90-percent biodegradability.[55])

A number of environmental agreements expressly confirm the right of parties to take more stringent measures individually or collectively. Examples are the 1973 Endangered Species Convention, the 1985 Ozone Layer Convention, and its 1987 Montreal Protocol. Under "framework" conventions, this right is frequently exercised in optional additional protocols concluded between some parties only. Within the 1979 Geneva *Convention on Long-range Transboundary Air Pollution,*[56] a ten-member "club" of countries first moved ahead in 1984 by declaring a voluntary 30-percent reduction of sulphur emissions[57]—a commitment not all of the 31 parties to the convention were prepared to share at that time. When the 30-percent reduction was formally adopted as a protocol to the convention at Helsinki in 1985, 21 states signed it.[58] During the negotiation of a further protocol on nitrogen oxides in 1987, a club of five like-minded states again pressed for a 30-percent reduction target;[59] and, even though the target did not become part of the protocol finally signed at Sofia in 1988,[60] twelve

of the protocol's 25 signatories eventually agreed to commit themselves to a voluntary 30-percent reduction.[61]

In each of these cases, the initiative taken by a "club within the club" played a pilot role in overall target-setting. It also had a bandwagon effect, with other parties climbing aboard as it gathered political momentum.

By calling for sulphur emission reductions by at least 30 percent, the 1985 Helsinki Protocol had introduced an "upwardly mobile" dynamic target. Since national reduction achievements and pledges are recorded annually, compared internationally and widely publicized, any over-achievement pays political dividends in terms of public attention and recognition.[62] As of 1988, twelve of the parties to the Helsinki Protocol thus reported that they had already reached the 30-percent target ahead of schedule, and ten parties announced that they would go on to reduce emissions by more than 50 percent *(See Figure 4 and Table 1).*[63]

A similar trend can be documented for the Montreal Protocol on ozone-depleting substances. While the 1987 meeting had after much bargaining settled for CFC reductions of only 50 percent until 1999,[64] the London Conference pledge by the 12-member European Community in March 1989 to 85 percent as soon as possible and 100 percent by the year 2000[65] led eventually to the Helsinki Declaration in May 1989—with 82 countries calling for a complete CFC phase-out by the end of the century.[66] This upward revision of the original bottomline was motivated partly by new scientific evidence of the "ozone hole,"[67] but media coverage and the worldwide publicity given to individual or collective pledges of over-achievement also proved influential.

Legally, there is ample room for stricter national rules on *bona fide* environmental grounds—provided they are non-discriminatory—under article XX of the *General Agreement on Tariffs and Trade* (GATT)[68] and under the 1979 Tokyo Round's *Agreement on Technical*

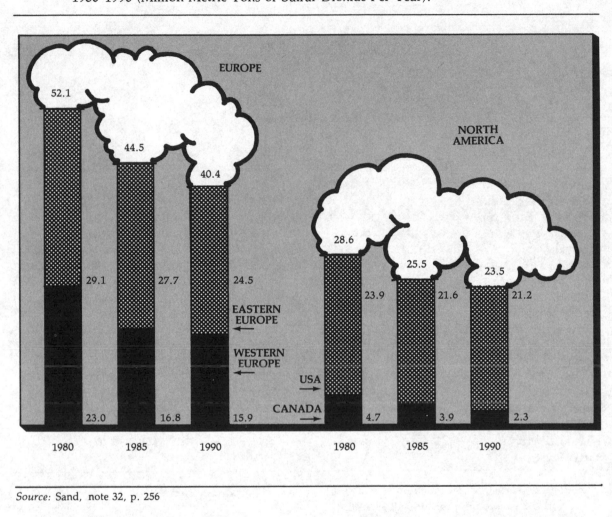

Figure 4. Trends in Total Man-Made Emissions of Sulfur Dioxide in Europe and North America, 1980-1990 (Million Metric Tons of Sulfur Dioxide Per Year).

Source: Sand, note 32, p. 256

Barriers to Trade.[69] The 1988 U.S.-Canadian *Free Trade Agreement* similarly recognizes environmental restrictions as ''legitimate domestic objectives.''[70]

In regional integration regimes, however, difficulties can arise. In the European Economic Community (EEC), for instance, there have been protracted quarrels over stricter national standards regarding fuel quality and engine emissions and over national subsidies for the purchase of ''clean cars.''[71] Although article

130T of the EEC Treaty as revised by the 1986 *Single European Act*[72] expressly authorizes more stringent national measures for environmental protection ''compatible with this treaty,'' and article 100A(4) enables member states to derogate from agreed harmonization measures for environmental reasons, a country planning to do so must first notify the EEC Commission (which may object in case of non-compatibility) so as to avoid arbitrary restraints of trade.[73] In the end, it is the trade regime that determines, if not the ''bottomline,'' at least the margin of

13

Table 1. Committed Sulphur Emission Reductions (in % of 1980 levels)

	ECE			EEC[3]		
	1993[1]	1995[2]	2000[2]	1993	1998	2003
Austria	−30	−69				
Belgium	−30	−48		−40	−60	−70
Bulgaria	−30					
Canada	−30	−36[4]	−33			
Czechoslovakia	−30	−31				
Denmark	−30	−57	−60	−34	−56	−67
Finland	−30	−52	−59			
France	−30	−57		−40	−60	−70
German Dem. Rep.	−30					
Germany, Fed. Rep.	−30	−69		−40	−60	−70
Greece				+6	+6	+6
Hungary	−30					
Ireland		+15		+25	+25	+25
Italy	−30			−27	−39	−63
Luxembourg	−30	−42		−40	−50	−60
Netherlands	−30	−62	−77	−40	−60	−70
Norway	−30	−51				
Poland			−29			
Portugal				+102	+135	+79
Spain		−6		0	−24	−27
Sweden	−30	−69	−80			
Switzerland	−30	−54	−51			
USSR	−30[5]					
United Kingdom			−41	−20	−40	−60
Yugoslavia		−30[6]				

1. Helsinki Protocol (all emission sources)
2. Declared over-achievements (all emission sources)
3. Directive on large combustion sources
4. Including −50 for 7 Eastern provinces
5. European part, including −30 for Byelorussian and Ukrainian republics
6. Slovenian republic only

tolerable asymmetries in the EEC's environmental regime.

Fast Tracks: How to Beat the Slowest-Boat Rule

Possibly the most serious drawback of the treaty method is the time lag between the drafting, adoption, and entry into force of standards. Besides the period of negotiation—which in the case of the Law of the Sea took fourteen years, and in the case of the Ozone Layer Convention more than three years—a treaty, once signed, must undergo a lengthy process of national ratification by the required minimum number of countries before it can become effective.

A 1971 study by the United Nations Institute for Training and Research (UNITAR) showed[74] that there are definite patterns of drag in treaty acceptance. Typically, multilateral treaties don't become effective until two to twelve years after formal agreement has been reached; the average "tempo of acceptance" for multilateral treaties, according to UNITAR, is about five years. While some—like the Law of the Sea Convention (which needs 60 ratifications)—have still not entered into force seven years after signature, most environmental treaties seem to be doing better. The Mediterranean Convention and the Ozone Layer Convention, for instance, took less than two years.

Possibly the most serious drawback of the treaty method is the time lag between the drafting, adoption, and entry into force of standards. The average "tempo of acceptance" for multilateral treaties is about five years.

Considering the need for rapid action on most environmental problems, even two years may be too long. The CFC-reduction rates agreed under the Montreal Protocol in September 1987 were already obsolete by the time the protocol entered into force and had to be revised by recourse to a "fast-track" procedure not foreseen in the treaty—the *Helsinki Declaration on the Protection of the Ozone Layer*, adopted in May 1989.[75]

The traditional ratification process and its notorious delays can, however, be bypassed in a number of ways. Among the bypass devices used in international environmental practice are provisional treaty application, various "soft-law" options, and delegated law-making.

Provisional Treaty Application. Pending the formal entry into force of an international

agreement, states may agree to bring it into operation on an interim basis. Provisional application is a recognized procedure under the Vienna Convention on the Law of Treaties;[76] a classical example is the 1947 *General Agreement on Tariffs and Trade* (GATT), which never legally came into force but has operated for more than 40 years now on the basis of a "protocol of provisional application."[77]

In the environmental field, the signatories to the 1979 Geneva *Convention on Long-range Transboundary Air Pollution*[78] also decided—by separate resolution—to "initiate, as soon as possible and on an interim basis, the provisional implementation of the convention" and to "carry out the obligations arising from the convention to the maximum extent possible pending its entry into force."[79] As a result, the executive body established by the convention took up its functions initially as "Interim Executive Body," holding regular annual meetings, creating subsidiary working groups, and the like, well before the convention took force in 1983.[80]

When adopting the first protocol under the convention in 1984 (on long-term financing of the *European Monitoring and Evaluation Program*, EMEP),[81] the signatories again decided by resolution—pending the entry into force of the protocol—"to contribute to financing of EMEP on a voluntary basis, in an amount equal to the mandatory contributions expected from them under the provisions of the protocol if all signatories had become parties."[82] Even though not all signatories complied, voluntary interim funding along these lines generated over $3.4 million, enabling the EMEP program to operate effectively[83] until 1988, when the protocol entered into force and contributions became mandatory.

The final act of the 1989 Basel Convention on Hazardous Wastes[84] took a similar, albeit more timid approach, with its resolution that "until such time as the convention comes into force and appropriate criteria are determined, all states refrain from activities which are inconsistent with the objectives and purposes of the Convention,"[85] and with other resolutions to establish preparatory technical working groups and an interim secretariat with voluntary funding. This, too, may be considered a provisional application, born of the signatories' determination to avoid a potential "anarchic hiatus" created by ratification delays.

Soft-Law Options. Alternatively, states may decide to forego treaty-making altogether and to recommend, by joint declaration, common rules of conduct—usually referred to as "soft law" to distinguish them from the "hard law" of formal legal agreements.[86] Environmental diplomacy has produced a wide variety of such declaratory instruments and resolutions. Their recognized practical advantage is that since they are not subject to national ratification, they can take instant effect. Their inherent risk, however, is precisely that lack of formality that makes them attractive as a short-cut. To illustrate the quandary, no sooner had the 1988 *Declaration on the 30 percent Reduction of Nitrogen Oxide Emissions*[87] been signed at Sofia on behalf of the Federal Republic of Germany, by its Minister for the Environment, than the State Secretary for Economic Affairs publicly questioned the legal force of the declaration.[88]

One of the most prolific soft-law-makers has been the Governing Council of the U.N. Environment Programme. Since 1978, it has addressed a whole series of "environmental law guidelines and principles" to states,[89] drafted in typical treaty language except for the copious use of "should" in place of "shall." Once adopted by *ad hoc* groups of experts nominated by governments, these provisions are normally approved by the UNEP Governing Council for submission to the U.N. General Assembly, which either incorporates them in a resolution (as in the case of the 1982 *World Charter for Nature*)[90] or, less solemnly, recommends them to states for use in the formulation of international agreements or national legislation (as in the case of the 1982 *Conclusions of the Study of Legal Aspects Concerning the Environment Related to Offshore Mining and Drilling Within the Limits of National Jurisdiction*).[91] In a number of cases, however, promulgation did not go beyond the level of a UNEP Governing Council decision (e.g., the 1980 *Provisions for Co-operation between States on Weather Modification*).[92]

Soft law may be "hardened" by later international practice. When the Government of Uganda, under gentle World Bank pressure, had to consult other Nile Basin countries on a proposed water use project for Lake Victoria in December 1983, it did so by way of reference to, among other documents, the 1978 UNEP *Principles of Conduct in the Field of the Environment for the Guidance of States in the Conservation and Harmonious Utilization of Natural Resources Shared by Two or More States.*[93] Three months later, the governments of Egypt and Sudan in their replies in turn referred to the guidelines as "jointly honored principles of cooperation," thereby quietly promoting them to the status of common regional standards.[94]

UNEP soft-law instruments have also served as forerunners of treaty law (as in the case of the 1985/1987 *Cairo Guidelines and Principles for the Environmentally Sound Management of Hazardous Wastes,*[95] which led up to the 1989 Basel Convention[96]) and as mandate for new mechanisms of intergovernmental co-operation (as in the case of the 1984 *Provisional Notification Scheme for Banned and Severely Restricted Chemicals*).[97] Environmental recommendations by other international organizations have played a similar role, especially those of the *Organisation for Economic Cooperation and Development* (OECD).

Even soft-law declarations by non-governmental expert groups may attain reference status, with or without intergovernmental blessing. The *International Law Association's* 1966 "Helsinki Rules" on the uses of the waters of international rivers[98] did just that. A more recent example is the set of *Proposed Legal Principles for Environmental Protection and Sustainable Development* appended to the 1987 Brundtland Report to the U.N. General Assembly.[99] Others are the guidelines for drinking-water quality[100] and ambient air quality[101] published under the World Health Organization's auspices: though drafted by *ad hoc* expert groups and never intergovernmentally adopted, they became a reference source for national standard-setting and a yardstick for comparative evaluation of environmental quality,[102] largely by virtue of the organization's prestige. Similarly, a number of worldwide technical standards for measuring environmental parameters are laid down and updated by the *International Organization for Standardization* (ISO). This organization ranks as "non-governmental"—even though more than 70 percent of its members are national public standards authorities—and its system of voting by correspondence is not subject to any diplomatic clearance or ratification.[103]

Delegated Law-Making. Another way of bypassing ratification is to delegate the powers to adopt and regularly amend "technical standards" to a specialized intergovernmental body. This technique was gradually developed and refined by several global and regional organizations that had to cope with frequent technological change: the *International Telecommunication Union* (ITU),[104] the *Universal Postal Union* (UPU),[105] and a number of European conventions on rail and road transport[106] each placed their international standards in separate "technical annexes" or "regulations" that are periodically revised in intergovernmental meetings without having to be ratified. Among the most advanced and smoothly functioning regulatory regimes so developed are the "international health regulations" of the *World Health Organization* (WHO)[107]; the "standard meteorological practices and procedures" of the *World Meteorological Organization* (WMO)[108]; the standards for facilitating international maritime traffic, enacted by the *International Maritime Organization* (IMO)[109]; and the international food standards of the *Codex Alimentarius Commission*, a joint technical body of WHO and the *Food and Agriculture Organization* of the United Nations (FAO).[110]

The efficacy of "ecostandards"[111] in expediting transnational decision-making is now

widely recognized.[112] Simplified (unratified) amendments of standards contained in technical annexes (as distinct from formal amendments of the main treaty provisions) are used in a wide range of global regimes for environmental standard-setting,[113] as well as in several regional agreements, including those for protecting the Baltic and the Mediterranean marine environment.[114]

Expeditious as it may be, bypassing ratification also means bypassing traditional parliamentary controls—raising the important question of whether delegated transnational standard-setting poses a threat to the democratic process.

Expeditious as it may be, bypassing ratification also means bypassing traditional parliamentary controls—raising the important question of whether delegated transnational standard-setting poses a "threat to the democratic process."[115] Different environmental regimes have come up with different answers to this question. One option is to entrust new control functions to a "supranational" parliamentary body such as the independently elected European Parliament, whose Environment Committee has begun to play an important watchdog role in the European Community's law-making process.[116] The alternative is to require national endorsement—still short of full ratification—for agreed-upon international standards, either through affirmative acceptance by governments (as in the case of the international food standards of the *Codex Alimentarius Commission*),[117] or by providing the possibility for dissenting states to "opt out" of a standard or amendment by a specified date (as stipulated, for instance, in the constitutions of the WHO, the WMO, the U.N. conventions on narcotic drugs, and in several international fisheries agreements).[118]

This opting-out procedure has already been applied in global pollution control. Consider the adoption and amendment of technical annexes under the 1944 *Chicago Convention on International Civil Aviation:*[119] Under articles 37 and 54 of the Convention, worldwide standards on aircraft noise and aircraft engine emissions have been laid down since 1981[120] by the Council of the *International Civil Aviation Organization* (ICAO). (The Council is elected every three years by the 162 member states represented in the ICAO Assembly; its 33 members[121] must take up full-time residence in Montreal at the organization's headquarters[122]— not unlike elected representatives in a national parliament.) Once adopted in the Council by a two-thirds majority vote,[123] an annex becomes mandatory—without ratification—for all states that do not within 60 days notify the Council of their intention to apply different national rules[124] and for all air traffic over the high seas.[125] This flexible "tacit consent" procedure, designed specifically to reconcile the divergent requirements of developed and developing nations,[126] makes it comparatively easy to adjust technical standards by majority decision without forcing complete uniformity.

The ICAO method of standard-setting is probably the closest thing to global environmental legislation developed so far—"a new category of international legal rules…which, strictly speaking, are neither customary nor contractual."[127] All the evidence suggests that this regime copes successfully both with the "bottomline" syndrome (by facilitating upward revision) and with the "slowest-boat" syndrome (by dispensing with ratification). The net result is, in Derek Bowett's words,[128] "[no] dramatic change in the basic rule of international law that states assume new obligations only with their consent, but rather a pattern of procedures for improving the chances of a decision of the majority (be it simple or two-thirds) of a 'legislative' character securing general consent."

INTERNATIONAL CIVIL AVIATION ORGANIZATION
INTERNATIONAL STANDARDS AND RECOMMENDED PRACTICES

ENVIRONMENTAL PROTECTION

ANNEX 16
TO THE CONVENTION ON INTERNATIONAL CIVIL AVIATION

VOLUME II
AIRCRAFT ENGINE EMISSIONS

FIRST EDITION—1981

This first edition of Volume II of Annex 16 was adopted by the Council on 30 June 1981 and becomes applicable on 18 February 1982.

(Amendment 1 of 4 March 1988 applicable 17 November 1988)

CHAPTER 2. TURBO-JET AND TURBOFAN ENGINES INTENDED FOR PROPULSION ONLY AT SUBSONIC SPEEDS

. . .

2.3 Gaseous Emissions

2.3.1   The provisions of 2.3.2 shall apply to engines whose rated output is greater than 26.7 kN and whose date of manufacture is on or after 1 January 1986.

2.3.2.   Gaseous emission levels when measured and computed in accordance with the procedures of Appendix 3 and converted to characteristic levels by the procedures of Appendix 6 shall not exceed the regulatory levels determined from the following formulas:

Hydrocarbons (HC):	$D_p/F\infty = 19.6$
Carbon monoxide (CO):	$D_p/F\infty = 118$
Oxides of nitrogen (NO_x):	$D_p/F\infty = 40 + 2\pi\infty$

D_p The mass of any gaseous pollutant emitted during the reference emissions landing and take-off cycle

$F\infty$ *Rated output.* For engine emissions purposes, the maximum power/thrust available for take-off under normal operating conditions at ISA sea level static conditions without the use of water injection as approved by the certificating authority. Thrust is expressed in kilonewtons.

$\pi\infty$ Reference pressure ratio—*Methods of measuring reference pressure ratio are given in Appendix 1.*

CONVENTION ON INTERNATIONAL CIVIL AVIATION
CONVENTION RELATIVE A L'AVIATION CIVILE INTERNATIONALE
CONVENIO SOBRE AVIACION CIVIL INTERNACIONAL

Pursuant to article 38,

—24 member states notified ICAO of their national *compliance* with the environmental protection standards of Annex 16/II as amended in 1988
(Argentina, Australia, Austria, Bahrain, Bangladesh, Barbados, Chile, Cuba, Cyprus, Denmark, El Salvador, Ethiopia, Fiji, Finland, Gambia, Kenya, Niger, Peru, Portugal, Solomon Islands, Sweden, Switzerland, Uruguay, Vanuatu)

—10 member states notified ICAO of national *differences* with regard to Annex 16/II as amended
(Canada, Federal Republic of Germany, Italy, Japan, Malawi, Netherlands, Saudi Arabia, Singapore, United Kingdom, United States of America)

—128 member states, after expiry of the notification period, are presumed to have *tacitly accepted* Annex 16/II as amended.

Article 38
Departures from international standards and procedures

Any State which finds it impracticable to comply in all respects with any such international standard or procedure, or to bring its own regulations or practices into full accord with any international standard or procedure after amendment of the latter, or which deems it necessary to adopt regulations or practices differing in any particular respect from those established by an international standard, shall give immediate notification to the International Civil Aviation Organization of the differences between its own practice and that established by the international standard. In the case of amendments to international standards, any State which does not make the appropriate amendments to its own regulations or practices shall give notice to the Council within sixty days of the adoption of the amendment to the international standard, or indicate the action which it proposes to take. In any such case, the Council shall make immediate notification to all other states of the difference which exists between one or more features of an international standard and the corresponding national practice of that State.

II. Innovations in Implementation

Once international standards have been set, institutions are needed to authorize or prohibit activities covered by the standards, and to impose sanctions against non-compliance. Unfortunately, most international environmental standards come without the necessary regulatory or judicial authority to apply them.

A number of recent initiatives—such as the Declaration of the Hague, signed by representatives of 24 countries in March 1989[129]—have called for "new institutional authority" to set and implement environmental standards. But without radical reforms in world government, transnational regimes for environmental governance still have to cope with a dual handicap:

First, in the absence of a supranational regulatory institution, only national institutions can license authorized activities (including assessment of their environmental impact). To the extent that these institutions apply agreed-upon international standards for this purpose, they may be said to act on behalf of the international community—by way of *dédoublement fonctionnel*, as Georges Scelle called it.[130] Yet, the relationship of these national licensing bodies with each other is strictly non-hierarchical, requiring far more complex procedures of reciprocity than needed when applying national standards.

Second, there is currently no compulsory jurisdiction for settling disputes over most multilateral environmental regimes. In most of the global agreements concluded since the 1970s, each party can prevent a case from being taken to arbitration or to the International Court of Justice in The Hague, since submission of disputes to third-party adjudication usually requires "common agreement."

Initially, these veto clauses were inserted at the insistence of the USSR and other East European countries that refused to accept compulsory third-party adjudication, deeming it an infringement on their sovereignty. More recently, in the wake of its rather painful court experience in the Nicaragua case,[131] the United States became the champion of the jurisdiction veto. In a bout of "Hague phobia," starting with the 1983 Cartagena *Convention for the Protection and Development of the Marine Environment of the Wider Caribbean Region*,[132] the U.S. State Department introduced a new variety of dispute-settlement clauses in all UNEP conventions that reserve each party's right to block third-party adjudication while leaving open an option to waive the veto right upon signing the treaty. This U.S.-inspired veto clause was also introduced—against strong resistance from 16 other Western countries favoring more stringent third-party adjudication[133]—in the 1985 *Vienna Convention for the Protection of the Ozone Layer*[134] and in the 1989 *Basel Convention on the Control of Transboundary Movements of Hazardous Wastes and their Disposal*.[135]

The first blow to the World Court's potential as a forum for environmental-dispute settlement had already been dealt in 1970 by Canada's reservation with regard to the Arctic Waters Pollution Prevention Act[136]—later reassurances by judges and friends of the court not withstanding.[137] Today, multilateral environmental agreements that can be enforced by compulsory international adjudication are the exception rather than the rule.[138] The imposition of sanctions for non-compliance thus requires different (non-hierarchic) approaches, again involving reciprocity. Further complicating matters, mutual obligations under multilateral agreements are more difficult to individualize than they are in bilateral disputes.[139]

Despite these complications, environmental regimes have "learned" to use alternative methods and institutions to ensure implementation of agreed-upon standards, as illustrated by the following examples.

Today, multilateral environmental agreements that can be enforced by compulsory international adjudication are the exception rather than the rule.

Alternatives to Supranational Regulation

The conspicuous absence of international regulatory institutions for environmental governance in no way prevented the proliferation of transnational regimes using a variety of regulatory mechanisms: environmental permits, environmental impact statements, environmental labels, etc. Experience shows that regulatory functions of this kind can very well be left to existing national bureaucracies. Usually, no new international bureaucratic superstructure is needed, as long as there is a workable measure of compatibility and mutual recognition of procedures, supported in practice by what political scientists describe as "epistemic"[140]

cooperation between specialists across national boundaries.

The conspicuous absence of international regulatory institutions for environmental governance in no way prevented the proliferation of transnational regimes using a variety of regulatory mechanisms.

Mutual Recognition. Rather than conferring licensing powers on an international body, many environmental agreements provide for the reciprocal recognition of licences and permits by competent national authorities. The only conditions are that these permits are properly authenticated and that certain agreed-upon standards are observed in granting them. Uniform sanitary and vaccination certificates have thus been issued over the past 40 years by national medical and veterinary services under the WHO *International Health Regulations*,[141] just as phytosanitary certificates for exports and re-exports have been under the 1951 *International Plant Protection Convention*.[142] National maritime and inland water authorities issue "international oil pollution prevention certificates" for ships pursuant to the 1973/1978 *Convention for the Prevention of Pollution from Ships* (MARPOL);[143] they also issue waste-disposal permits for substances listed on the "grey lists" of at least ten global and regional agreements aimed at preventing marine and inland water pollution, starting with the 1972 London *Convention on the Prevention of Marine Pollution by Dumping of Waste and Other Matter*.[144] Under the 1989 *Basel Convention on the Control of Transboundary Movements of Hazardous Wastes and Their Disposal*,[145] waste-export notifications and authorizations will also be issued exclusively by national authorities.

In the chemical industry, international trade depends largely on reciprocal recognition schemes. For example, under the World Health Organization's *Certification Scheme on the Quality of Pharmaceutical Products Moving in International Commerce*[146]—introduced in 1975 and now applied by 125 countries—the exporting state's health authority is required to certify upon request whether the manufacturer has been found on inspection to comply with defined standards of practice in the manufacture and quality control of drugs. Some countries have gone further toward harmonizing their reference procedures. Examples include the chemical test guidelines and principles of good laboratory practice laid down by the *Organisation for Economic Cooperation and Development* (OECD);[147] the 1970 *Convention for the Mutual Recognition of Inspections in Respect of the Manufacture of Pharmaceutical Products*,[148] adopted within the framework of the *European Free Trade Association* (EFTA) in Geneva but also followed by several non-EFTA countries; and the 1979 "sixth amendment" to the European Community's *Directive on the Approximation of Laws, Regulations and Administrative Provisions Relating to Classification, Packaging and Labelling of Dangerous Substances*,[149] also followed by a number of countries outside the EEC. The basis of these regimes invariably remains one of reciprocal acceptance of national certification.[150]

Similarly, the 1973 Washington *Convention on International Trade in Endangered Species of Wild Fauna and Flora* (CITES)[151] established worldwide trade controls based on mandatory permits and certificates covering the export, import, and re-export of plant and animal species or products listed in the Convention appendices. Yet, these permits are not issued by an international institution. Instead, the entire CITES regime relies on the mutual recognition and verification of national permits, issued by designated authorities in each of the 106 member states. The international secretariat merely provides coordination and "switchboard" services.

The CITES approach has, of course, numerous historical antecedents in international relations—from seaworthiness and airworthiness certificates for ships and aircraft, to the classification and labelling of alcoholic beverages. The incentive for governments to participate in any such regime (and the primary sanction of the regime) is its reciprocity, and the practical economic advantages this offers to the participating state, especially where compliance facilitates international communications or the export of certain products.[152]

An example is the licensing of imported cars in Europe under the 1958 Geneva *Agreement concerning the Adoption of Uniform Conditions of Approval and Reciprocal Recognition of Approval for Motor Vehicle Equipment and Parts*.[153] Under this regime, authorizations for marketing new cars are based on "type-approval" of vehicle models, which in turn depends on, among other things, certified compliance with uniform technical criteria for engine emissions. Even though these emission standards are harmonized internationally and periodically updated by the Inland Transport Committee of the U.N. Economic Commission for Europe (ECE)—again, under a "simplified" procedure of delegated law-making without ratification, requiring approval by only two of the 22 member states to bring a technical regulation or amendment into force[154]—vehicles are licensed by designated national agencies, not by an international body. A licence issued by one agency is officially recognized in all other participating countries, which makes the system particularly attractive to car manufacturers as a shortcut to foreign markets. (Indeed, the Japanese Government maintains permanent observer status in the ECE Working Party concerned.) At the same time, the ECE regional standards so applied are increasingly becoming models for national licensing in other countries outside of Europe.[155] *De facto*, therefore, the geographical scope of the regime is expanding well beyond the treaty's membership.

Model Diffusion. Harmonization of environmental standards may also occur informally as foreign regulatory models are voluntarily adopted. Many developing countries today

UNITED NATIONS
ECONOMIC COMMISSION FOR EUROPE

AGREEMENT

CONCERNING THE ADOPTION OF UNIFORM CONDITIONS OF APPROVAL AND RECIPROCAL RECOGNITION OF APPROVAL FOR MOTOR VEHICLE EQUIPMENT AND PARTS

done at Geneva on 20 March 1958

Regulation No. 49* Revision 1
(entry into force: 1 October 1990)

UNIFORM PROVISIONS CONCERNING THE APPROVAL OF COMPRESSION IGNITION (C.I.) ENGINES AND VEHICLES EQUIPPED WITH C.I. ENGINES WITH REGARD TO THE EMISSIONS OF GASEOUS POLLUTANTS BY THE ENGINE

1. SCOPE

    This Regulation applies to the emission of gaseous pollutants from C.I. engines used for driving motor vehicles having a design speed exceeding 25 km/h of categories M_1 having a total mass exceeding 3.5 tonnes, M_2, M_3, N_1, N_2 and N_3.**
    . . .

5.2 Specifications concerning the emission of pollutants

    The emission of pollutants by the engine submitted for testing shall be measured by the method described in annex 4. Other methods may be approved if it is found that they yield equivalent results. The emissions of the carbon monoxide, the emissions of the hydrocarbons and the emissions of the oxides of nitrogen contained shall not exceed the amounts shown in the table below:

Mass of carbon monoxide (CO) grammes per kWh	Mass of hydro-carbons (HC) grammes per kWh	Mass of oxides of nitrogen (NO_x) grammes per kWh
11.2	2.4	14.4

---

*UN/ECE Regulation No. 49 on emissions from diesel engines is currently applied in the following countries: *Belgium; Czechoslovakia; France; Finland, Germany* (East and West); *Hungary; Italy; Luxembourg; Netherlands; Romania; USSR; United Kingdom;* and *Yugoslavia. Australia* and *New Zealand* apply UN/ECE Regulations No. 49 unilaterally. Pursuant to EEC Directives 88/76, 88/77 and 88/436, provisions corresponding to Revision 1 of UN/ECE Regulation No. 49 will become mandatory in all 12 member countries of the *European Community* in October 1990. *Austria* and *Switzerland* have announced stricter national emission standards for diesel engines; whereas *Norway* and *Sweden* will align their requirements on 1990 U.S. standards.
**I.e., diesel-fuelled passenger cars, trucks and buses.

admit imported chemical products without national evaluation if the product was duly licensed in its country of origin—thereby relying on the presumed effectiveness of foreign controls. On the other hand, several European countries unabashedly borrow U.S. federal or California state standards to upgrade their national legislation on automobile emissions.[156]

The international transfer of innovative norms and institutions, a transcultural process described as *mimesis* by Arnold Toynbee,[157] follows patterns of geographical diffusion quite similar to the spread of technological innovations.[158] Some social geographers have even drawn parallels with the spread of contagious diseases[159]—vindicating a metaphor already used by Goethe, in *Faust*:

> *"All rights and laws are still transmitted*
> *like an eternal sickness of the race,*
> *from generation unto generation fitted*
> *and shifted round from place to place."*[160]

One legislative innovation that has spread widely is the "environmental impact assessment" (EIA) procedure first introduced by the 1969 U.S. National Environmental Policy Act.[161] While attempts to internationalize the procedure through a treaty—advocated by U.S. Senator Claiborne Pell since 1978[162]—were manifestly unsuccessful and never progressed beyond a "soft law" declaration in the U.N. Environment Programme,[163] the underlying concept of the legislation rapidly and quite informally became a model for at least 30 countries worldwide. EIA now is a commonplace legal term not only in English-speaking countries from Australia to Zambia,[164] but also as *declaración de efecto ambiental* in the 1974 Colombian Code of Renewable Natural Resources and Environment Protection,[165] or *evaluación de impacto ambiental* in Spain's 1986 Royal Decree on EIA;[166] as *étude d'impact sur l'environnement* in the 1976 French Nature Conservation Act[167] (followed by similar provisions in other French-speaking countries, such as the 1983 Algerian Act on Environment Protection[168]); and as *Umweltverträglichkeitsprüfung* (UVP) in the 1990 West German EIA

Act[169] (based on a 1985 European Community *Directive on the Assessment of the Effects of Certain Public and Private Projects on the Environment*[170]), and in recent (1988) East German legislation.[171] Here again, parallels may be drawn with worldwide diffusion of other institutional models—notably, the "TVA syndrome" in river basin management.[172]

Another widely diffused model of this kind is the concept of a pollution tax or financial charge pro-rated to the volume of pollutant emissions. Originally developed (since 1904) as "effluent fees" for regional pollution control by water management associations in the Ruhr River Basin,[173] emission charges have since been introduced in many other regions and countries and applied to a wide range of other environmental issues. The basic idea is to levy a disincentive charge on specified economic activities, depending on how much environmental harm they do, and to earmark the proceeds from the charge for specific countermeasures.[174] Effluent charges for water pollution are now part of national law in both Germanies and elsewhere in Western Europe (the Netherlands, France, Italy),[175] as well as in Eastern Europe (Czechoslovakia, Hungary, Poland).[176] They have been proposed for adoption in the United States and the USSR.[177] Landing charges for aircraft noise, pro-rated according to engine type or aircraft weight, are levied in Japan and at several West European airports.[178] Since March 1988, all domestic air traffic in Sweden is subject to a pro-rated charge on aircraft engine emissions of nitrogen oxides and hydrocarbons.[179]

Surprisingly, emission charges seem to function both in market economies and in centrally planned economies: the (East) German Democratic Republic first introduced a "dust and gaseous emissions fee" on industrial enterprises emitting air pollutants in excess of specified levels, starting experimentally in two of the most polluted districts in 1969 and extending the system country-wide by legislation in 1973.[180] Hungary and Poland followed.[181] In 1985, France enacted a "para-fiscal air pollution tax" on all large fossil-fuel combustion sources emitting more than 2,500 metric tons of sulphur dioxide per year (some 480 plants representing about two thirds of total sulphur emissions in the country), taxed at 130 francs per metric ton sulphur dioxide (about two cents per kilogram), with the proceeds going to anti-pollution investments in the industries concerned.[182] From 1990 onwards, the French tax will be raised to 150 francs per ton and extended to industrial emissions of nitrogen oxides (NO_x). Finland enacted a whole package of "environmental taxes" on fossil fuels as part of its 1990 budget legislation,[183] and similar measures—including a new charge on carbon dioxide (CO_2) emissions at the rate of 25 öre (about 4 cents) per kilogram CO_2—are under discussion in Sweden.[184] This impressive progress aside, none of the existing emission charges today are considered steep enough to achieve the full "polluter-pays" effect postulated in welfare economics. None will, in other words, internalize all social costs generated by a pollution source.[185] Rather, their avowed function is to raise para-fiscal revenue through environmentally rational penalties.[186]

None of the existing emission charges today are considered steep enough to achieve the full "polluter-pays" effect postulated in welfare economics. Rather, their avowed function is to raise para-fiscal revenue through environmentally rational penalties.

A more recent example of transnational diffusion is the "environmental label" for consumer products first introduced in the Federal Republic of Germany in 1978.[187] There, an expert jury under the auspices of the Federal Environment Ministry awards to consumer products an official environmental quality label, based on the international logo of the United Nations Environment Programme and popularly known as the "blue angel."[188] *(See Figure 5.)* Once commercial users pay a license fee to the non-governmental National Institute for Quality Assurance and Certification (RAL), they can use the label in advertising and packaging on products ranging from low-emission oil combustion units to "environmentally benign" (recycled) toilet paper.[189] The scheme turned out to be highly popular and successful—lawsuits by disgruntled competitors notwithstanding[190]—and currently some 3500 products on the market bear the blue angel mark.[191] Similar systems of product labelling and licensing, partly based on the West German experience, were introduced in 1989 both in Canada (EcoLogo)[192] and in Japan (EcoMark).[193] In November 1989, the Nordic Council of Ministers adopted a joint environmental label for consumer products ("miljömärkt") to be used in all Scandinavian countries, based on national certification following along common guidelines.[194]

In each of these schemes, the private sector participates through representatives of non-governmental industrial, environmental, and consumer protection associations. In some, non-governmental institutions are empowered to do the licensing. In the Federal Republic of Germany, most anti-pollution equipment for motor vehicles and stationary emission sources is certified under contract by regional engineering societies known as TÜV (*Technische Ueberwachungs-Vereine*, or technical inspection associations).[195] Similar non-governmental inspection services for motor vehicles exist in Belgium and Sweden, which (jointly with governmental inspectorates from other European countries) participate in the *International Motor Vehicle Inspection Committee*. In Norway, technical and environmental certification of offshore mining platforms is carried out by a private company *(Det Norske Veritas)*, following the century-old practice of classifying seaworthy ships, initiated by insurance companies such as Lloyd's.[196] The Geneva-based *Société Générale de Surveillance* (SGS), through its various subsidiaries and affiliates in 140 countries, also

Figure 5. Environmental Product Labels

Blue Angel West Germany, 1978

EcoMark Japan, 1989

EcoLogo Canada, 1989

Environment Mark Nordic Council, 1989

Source: Sand, note 32, p. 256.

provides inspection services for environmental quality certification under commercial contracts.[197]

To avoid unfair trade practices, arrangements for mutual recognition of national environmental labels, possibly including harmonized standards and procedures of product selection and identification, will become necessary.

Wider diffusion of these institutional models is bound to raise transnational problems. Already more than 10 percent of the current environmental product labels in the Federal Republic of Germany are held by foreign firms (including 14 from the Netherlands, 11 from Austria, 33 from ten other West European countries, plus some Japanese car manufacturers and American chemical companies)[198]—and the trend is rising in anticipation of the free-trade regime of the 1992 European Common Market. Conversely, West German exports carrying the "blue angel" are reportedly gaining new market shares in the United Kingdom and other countries with environmentally conscious consumers.[199] To avoid unfair trade practices, arrangements for mutual recognition of national environmental labels, possibly including harmonized standards and procedures of product selection and identification, will become necessary. For instance, since the West German jury already allows the applicant's home state (Länder) authorities to participate in the proceedings,[200] why not open the procedure to competent foreign authorities where applicable?

Alert Diffusion. Transnational diffusion of regulatory experience is particularly important in environmental risk management. Some 70,000 chemicals are in common use today, with 500 to 1,000 new compounds added every year. While very little is known yet about the toxicity of almost two thirds of these,[201] information is available on national regulatory action concerning chemicals already considered environmentally harmful or hazardous. Following a 1982 General Assembly Resolution,[202] the U.N. secretariat regularly publishes a "consolidated list" of products whose consumption or sale have been banned, withdrawn, severely restricted, or not approved by governments. The 4th (1990) edition lists some 400 chemicals and 300 pharmaceuticals.

Following regional initiatives by the Organisation for Economic Cooperation and Development, and inspired in part by earlier U.S. federal legislation,[203] the Governing Council of the U.N. Environment Programme in 1984 adopted a "provisional notification scheme" for banned or severely restricted chemicals, requiring countries to exchange standard warnings when exporting any of these products.[204] Further elaborated by the 1987 London *Guidelines for the Exchange of Information on Chemicals in International Trade*,[205] the scheme is administered by UNEP's Geneva-based International Register of Potentially Toxic Chemicals and currently implemented by 75 countries. Related provisions are found in the *International Code of Conduct on the Distribution and Use of Pesticides* adopted by the Food and Agriculture Organization of the United Nations in 1985.[206] (Both the UNEP and the FAO procedure were amended in 1989 to include the requirement of "prior informed consent," under which participating importing countries will have to give their express approval before hazardous chemicals can be brought in.[207])

Information diffusion of this kind serves as a danger signal to importing countries, especially with regard to the 50 to 100 "red flag" chemicals currently banned by more than ten states. While this process may be tantamount to black-listing, no international regulatory action is involved since both the consolidated UN list and the UNEP/OECD schemes are based entirely on national regulatory decisions in the countries concerned.[208]

A similar notification procedure debuted under article 5 of the CITES treaty.[209] Besides the Convention's international "black" and "grey" lists of endangered species (appendices I and II), there is a separate third appendix in which each member state may list any species or taxa whose export it wishes to ban or control for national reasons. Unlike the listing of species in appendices I and II, which requires international agreement by a two-thirds majority vote, appendix III listings are made by simple unilateral notification to the CITES secretariat, which in turn communicates it to all other member states with a request to adjust their trade controls accordingly. Although originally not accorded much weight, recourse to appendix III has increased over the years. By 1989, 249 taxa were listed.[210]

In addition, as a matter of practice gradually developed in treaty administration, the CITES secretariat has begun to notify all parties whenever a member state announces a national ban on exports or imports—over and above the controls required by the treaty—so as to solicit international enforcement assistance.[211] While such calls are issued voluntarily—and are not always viewed kindly by other Parties, in view of the extra administrative burden involved[212]—they rarely go unheeded, and they are duly included in the enforcement instructions given by most governments to their trade-control authorities. Precautionary diffusion of foreign restrictions thus tends to produce the desired result, even though the system is not strictly mandatory.

Epistemic Networks. A crucial factor for the success of environmental agreements is direct permanent contact among the national agencies, groups, and individuals entrusted with implementation. Reference is often made to the role of "technical elites"[213] or "epistemic communities"[214] to explain consensus-building in the negotiation of international agreements. Experience with environmental regimes suggests that *epistemes*—defined as "a set of shared symbols and references, mutual expectations and a mutual predictability of intentions"[215]—may be even more important during implementation.

A common feature of mutual recognition schemes is their reliance on a permanent network of national administrators, designated as the official channel for transnational communication and verification. CITES[216] established a network of "management authorities" and "scientific authorities," mostly consisting of wildlife management officers and wildlife biologists. The WHO, UNEP, and OECD schemes to control trade in chemicals[217] (as well as the future Basel Convention network for hazardous wastes[218]) rely on designated public health officials and government chemists. The ECE motor vehicle certification system[219] works through licensing agencies usually staffed by automotive engineers. Monitoring under the Transboundary Air Pollution Convention[220] is carried out by the EMEP network of stations and laboratories,[221] most of which are part of national meteorological services. Often, the transnational expert communities so established include non-governmental sectors—industry, research institutions, and competent environmental groups. In each case, the common professional background of participants tends to foster a distinct "epistemic" solidarity across frontiers—the old boys' network.

As a rule, authority for licensing or monitoring decisions of the kind described here (whether they concern imported chemicals, cars, wildlife products, or meteorological data) is delegated to officials at an intermediate technical level. For efficiency's sake, their communications with each other and with the international secretariats concerned are usually direct, skirting national departmental hierarchies and virtually bypassing diplomatic channels. Since transnational contacts enhance the professional status of participants, they create strong incentives for continuing and expanding international agreements. Just as mutual confidence and "cognitive convergence"[222] among specialists develops when treaties are prepared and negotiated, technocratic solidarity among those who monitor compliance feeds back into the national evaluation and into the further development of environmental regimes. It also makes cheating in treaty implementation more difficult and can prevent or at least defuse disputes.

Alternatives to Intergovernmental Litigation

When evaluating the implementation and effectiveness of international agreements, lawyers tend to focus on judicial or quasi-judicial enforcement, in particular through the principle of state responsibility (now being codified by the U.N. International Law Commission).[223] The growing literature on state responsibility for environmental harm is usually traced back to the 1941 U.S.-Canadian *Trail Smelter* arbitration.[224] In practice, though, intergovernmental litigation of the Trail Smelter type is rare and plays little or no role in the implementation of multilateral treaties and standards. Indeed, the 1979 Geneva *Convention on Long-range Transboundary Air Pollution* expressly excludes the question of state liability for damage.[225]

Intergovernmental liability suits don't seem to be a promising way of enforcing multilateral environmental agreements.

For at least two reasons, intergovernmental liability suits don't seem to be a promising way of enforcing multilateral environmental agreements. First, unlike the bilateral Trail Smelter case, which concerned a single point source in Canada causing instant harm to identified victims nearby in the United States, today's multilateral regimes increasingly deal with the long-range (up to several thousand miles) and long-term (up to several generations) effects of multiple pollutants from a variety of sources that are difficult to pin down. Second, the time-cost of the Trail Smelter case, which from the first claims in 1926 to the final arbitral award in 1941 took a solid 15 years, was far higher than most environmental cases today can afford.

In spite of these limitations, international lawyers continue to extrapolate "principles" from this venerable single precedent, like good generals rehearsing the wars of yesteryear. Yet, most transnational environmental regimes have learned to avoid the adversarial state-liability approach; instead, they have used or developed different methods of ensuring compliance with treaty obligations. A number of alternative channels and mechanisms are available for this purpose, including some promising innovative approaches.

Local Remedies. The Trail Smelter case developed into an international arbitration only because a deadlock arose between local legal rules: While nothing prevented American air pollution victims from bringing a private law suit in Canada, the local Canadian courts in the 1930s would have refused—under an ancient House of Lords rule[226]—to take jurisdiction over suits based on damage to foreign land.[227] On the other hand, Washington state law did not permit a foreign corporation to acquire smoke easements on Washington land.[228] Had these domestic procedural obstacles been removed by more flexible rules governing foreign parties, the case would probably never have moved to intergovernmental arbitration.

More recent environmental case law demonstrates that numerous local legal remedies are available to defuse transboundary problems and to resolve the apparent conflicts between divergent legal systems. For example, in the 1957 case of *Poro vs. Lorraine Basin Coalmines*,[229] which involved air pollution from a power plant in France harming residents in West Germany, a German appeal court chose to determine damages "in accordance with the law most favorable to the plaintiff"—in this instance, the French Civil Code.[230] Significantly, the bulk of disputes over transboundary pollution damage along the Rhine River since 1975 were resolved by local remedies, either through national courts or by out-of-court settlements and insurance.[231]

Of course, this approach also requires a degree of mutual recognition to be given to foreign decisions—as, for instance, under the Brussels (1968) and Lugano (1988) Conventions on jurisdiction and enforcement of judgments in civil and commercial matters in Europe.[232] There must be certain guarantees for the status of foreign parties in local judicial and administrative proceedings, as under the 1974 *Nordic Environmental Protection Convention*[233] or the *Outline Convention on Transfrontier Cooperation between Territorial Communities or Authorities* adopted in 1980 by the Council of Europe.[234] The *Recommendations on Equal Right of Access and Non-discrimination in Relation to Transfrontier Pollution*, adopted in 1976 and 1977 by the Organisation for Economic Cooperation and Development,[235] played a pilot role in this field; and a draft "convention on environmental impact assessment in a transboundary context," now under preparation in the U.N. Economic Commission for Europe,[236] aims at harmonizing procedures for environmental planning and decision-making in border regions. Opening local remedies to foreign parties can go a long way toward de-escalating transboundary disputes to their ordinary neighborhood level.[237]

Complaints and Custodial Action. As an alternative to legal action against the responsible party, recourse to a non-judicial international institution may provide a first-choice remedy when environmental agreements are infringed. Under the non-compliance procedure currently being developed for the 1987 *Montreal Protocol on Substances That Deplete the Ozone Layer,*[238] complaints by one or more parties will initially be filed with the UNEP secretariat, which will gather additional information and eventually submit the file to a five-party "Implementation Committee."[239] But even though this proposed procedure was very cautiously defined as non-judicial and non-confrontational, a number of states already cautioned that "any supra-national body to review data would be

unacceptable,"[240] which bodes ill for the chances of such a mechanism.

A much bolder step toward collective compliance control was taken by the 1957 Rome Treaty establishing the *European Economic Community* (EEC).[241] Article 155 made the EEC Commission the guardian of the treaty's implementation, and article 169 empowered it to initiate proceedings against any member state in case of infringements, sanctioned if necessary by formal action in the European Court of Justice at Luxembourg.[242] Over the past ten years, this "custodial" procedure has become one of the most important means of enforcing EEC environmental standards.

The EEC infringement proceedings[243] comprise three stages: As a first step, the Commission sends "letters of formal notice" to member states that fail to enact or apply a Community directive, or to report on its enactment or application. After giving the member state an opportunity to respond, the Commission can next render a "reasoned opinion" confirming the infringement in light of all the facts gathered. If the member state still doesn't comply, the Commission may then refer the matter to the European Court of Justice. During 1988, the Commission issued 93 letters of formal notice, 71 reasoned opinions, and 11 references to the court concerning infringements of EEC environmental directives (some 70 of which were in force at that time).[244] A country-by-country comparison of infringement proceedings pending at the end of 1989 is given in Table 2.

What may be the most significant feature of this procedure is mentioned nowhere in the treaty and evolved only gradually during its implementation. More than half of the infringement proceedings initiated against member states were based not on the Commission's own monitoring of compliance but on citizen complaints—from private individuals, associations (such as Greenpeace and Friends of the Earth), or municipalities.[245] As a result of public information on the complaints procedure

Table 2. Proceedings for Infringements of EEC Environmental Directives

| | EEC Commission action pursuant to Art. 169 pending as of 31. 12. 1989 | | | EEC Court decisions pursuant to Art. 169 against member states |
	Letters of notice	Reasoned opinions	References to EEC Court	(1981–1989)
Belgium	27	8	11	13
Denmark	5	—	—	1
France	28	6	7	1
Germany, Fed. Rep.	13	8	8	2
Greece	37	5	3	—
Ireland	16	5	—	—
Italy	17	16	7	8
Luxembourg	9	2	1	—
Netherlands	18	5	2	4
Portugal	10	4	—	—
Spain	45	9	3	—
United Kingdom	18	8	5	—
TOTALS	242	76	44	29

Source: Control of the Application of Community Law on Environment, A First Commission Report, *EEC Information Memo* P/90/5 (8 February 1990), Annex 2; and *Official Journal of the European Communities* No. C 330 (30 December 1989) p. 38.

and the establishment of a "complaints registry" within the Commission secretariat in Brussels, the number of environmental complaints rose dramatically—from 10 in 1982 to 190 in 1988 and to 460 in 1989.[246] While complaints are usually based on local non-compliance with EEC standards, some have wider effects: a single complaint by a resident in one of the United Kingdom's two non-attainment areas with regard to the 1980 EEC *Directive on Air Quality Limit Values and Guide Values for Sulphur Dioxide and Suspended Particulates*[247] thus triggered a Commission investigation that led to infringement proceedings against seven member states.[248]

Significantly, the EEC has no powers of physical enforcement comparable to those of a national government. Although virtually all of

the more than 30 judgments rendered by the European Court of Justice in environmental infringement proceedings since 1982 went against the defendant member states and upheld the Commission's opinion, not all led to compliance. In the 1988 case of *Commission vs. Kingdom of Belgium*,[249] for instance, the court noted that Belgium had failed to fulfil its obligations under article 171 of the treaty by refusing, in defiance of earlier (1982) judgments of the court, to adopt the measures necessary to implement four EEC directives on waste disposal. The mere opening of EEC action can, however, have internal political and economic consequences in member states. In the United Kingdom, the government's plans for privatization of local water management agencies were stalled in part because of pending EEC infringement proceedings, when it turned out that some areas scheduled for privatization did not meet EEC water quality standards.[250] As a result of this growing impact on local environmental quality, the "custodial action" procedure of the EEC Commission has evolved from a three-stage to a four-stage process: the optional first stage in most cases is now a citizen complaint.[251]

Environmental Audits. Besides judicial review, international organizations have developed other forms of compliance control. Probably the body with the most such experience is the *International Labour Organization* (ILO), which has enacted and monitored a long line of multilateral conventions since the 1920s— ranging from bans on white lead paint and other occupational health hazards, to workplace protection from air pollution, radiation, and toxic chemicals.[252] All these conventions contain provisions on dispute settlement that allow states to initiate complaints and *ad hoc* inquiries against other states for not observing the treaty. However, a detailed study of ILO's enforcement record over more than sixty years shows that this adversarial procedure was used only rarely and then mostly for political potshots.[253] Instead, ILO member states developed an entirely different procedure that turned out to be far more effective in enforcing compliance: annual or biennial reporting by governments, combined with regular auditing by an independent technical Committee of Experts to ascertain compliance in each member state, followed by public debate of these audited reports by the Conference Committee on the Application of Conventions and Recommendations.[254]

Over the years, the ILO "auditing" system— with the active participation of both trade unions and employers' associations—has turned into a worldwide public hearing that clearly induces more compliance by governments than the threat of any intergovernmental legal action would. The U.N. *Commission on Human Rights* applies a similar procedure of country reports and public hearings,[255] in which non-governmental organizations (such as Amnesty International) play an active role.

In the environmental field, the biennial Conference of the Parties to the *Convention on International Trade in Endangered Species of Wild Fauna and Flora* (CITES)[256] has become a forum for international review of compliance with the treaty, again with massive NGO support. Similarly, reviews of treaty implementation by parties to the *Convention on Long-Range Transboundary Air Pollution*[257] and its protocols are carried out and published regularly by the Executive Body for the Convention.[258]

In all these cases, periodic audits of compliance with agreed-upon international standards are well established. Essential to this process is publicity. It facilitates collective review and mutual accountability[259] by all member states and, even more important, exposes governmental compliance reports to scrutiny by non-governmental groups and, through them, by the public.[260]

The concept of environmental auditing has also been taken up directly by such non-governmental groups as Friends of the Earth[261] and by industry. Several major transnational corporations—at least partly in response to the Bhopal shock—now carry out regular environmental audits to ensure that regulatory requirements and long-term environmental liabilities (such as legal waste-disposal duties) are accurately reflected in their subsidiaries' balance-sheets.[262] In November 1988, the Executive Board of the *International Chamber of Commerce* (ICC) adopted a position paper on environmental auditing for business organizations, reflecting experience in countries and companies where the practice is already well established.[263] A fundamental difference remains, however, between the more limited scope of auditing as an internal business management technique and the idea of public review, which emerges as the key element of the international environmental audit procedures presented here. Inherent in the latter is public disclosure as a means of ensuring democratic control over the implementation of agreed-upon international standards.

Considering the clear need to make environmental controls preventive rather than corrective, now may be the time to envisage a global auditing body that would periodically evaluate the performance of states and organizations in complying with their international obligations.

One strong point of environmental audits is timing. Audits can make a difference *before* things have gone seriously wrong—unlike traditional judicial review mechanisms based on liability, which can only intervene after the fact. Considering the clear need to make environmental controls preventive rather than corrective, now may be the time to envisage a global auditing body that would periodically evaluate the performance of states and organizations in complying with their international obligations. Rather than relying on *ad hoc* review by a tribunal, where "action" would inevitably turn into confrontation, it may be preferable to assign this function to a permanent intergovernmental body—such as the *United Nations Trusteeship Council*, as recently suggested by Maurice Strong, Secretary General of the U.N. Conference on Environment and Development.[264] As in the field of standard-setting and regulation, more imaginative approaches to compliance control are needed today than those drawn from outdated legal textbooks. An obvious and largely untapped source is the rich procedural experience of existing international institutions.[265]

Outlook: A View from the Anthill

In the current international debate on environmental priorities in the face of global change, far too many hopes seem pinned on some new utopia of world government. It is most unlikely that problems of this dimension—such as climate modification—can be resolved by organizational restructuring alone, nor for that matter by yet another epic codification *à la* Law of the Sea. Given the urgency of the task, the most expedient and most economic course of action would be to activate and accelerate all available international machinery without waiting for new global institutions.

Making environmental standard-setting and implementation coherent will require more than further coordination within the United Nations family of organizations.

The obvious disadvantage of relying on the existing structure is its sheer complexity. We are dealing with an aggregate, rather than a system, of multiple environmental regimes. Ernst Haas has compared it to an anthill,[266] but the analogy may be euphemistic considering the well-organized hierarchies of social insects. Making environmental standard-setting and

implementation coherent will require more than further coordination within the United Nations family of organizations; indeed, the whole range of global and regional institutions must be involved. An impressive start in this direction has already been made by the small "Centre for Our Common Future" set up in Geneva in 1988 to oversee follow-up to the Brundtland report.[267]

An advantage of the present structure—and one that hopefully sets it apart from the stereotype of insect societies—is its openness and adaptiveness to change. Any new institutional arrangements for environmental governance should seek to preserve and enhance this capacity. Practical devices for this purpose include the built-in review schedules that have appeared in a number of recent environmental agreements:

• The 1987 *Montreal Protocol on Substances That Deplete the Ozone Layer* stipulated that "beginning in 1990, and at least every four years thereafter, the Parties shall assess the control measures...on the basis of available scientific, environmental, technical and economic information."[268] Four assessment panels, coordinated by an intergovernmental "Open-ended Working Group,"[269] were set up in 1989 and will report to the second meeting of the Parties in June 1990.

• The 1988 *Sofia Protocol to the Convention on Long-range Transboundary Air Pollution* provides for regular reviews of the agreement, starting no later than one year after its entry into force. It also says that negotiations on further steps must start no later than six months after entry into force and "[take] into account the best available scientific and technological developments."[270] In anticipation of this process, an intergovernmental "Working Group on Abatement Strategies" began to meet in 1989 and will report to the Executive Body for the Convention in November 1991.

• The 1989 *Basel Convention on the Control of Transboundary Movements of Hazardous Wastes and Their Disposal* has scheduled an evaluation of the treaty's effectiveness three years after its entry into force and at least every six years thereafter. The evaluation mandate includes the possible "adoption of a complete or partial ban of transboundary movements of hazardous wastes and other wastes in light of the latest scientific, environmental, technical and economic information."[271]

This new generation of all-out reviews—mirrored in the broad remit of the U.N. *Conference on Environment and Development* in 1992[272]—clearly amounts to more than a routine inspection and maintenance service.[273] If the mandate of a review is policy re-orientation in light of future knowledge and experience, it must include the option of consequential institutional change. What emerges, then, is indeed close to the new "fluid" model of environmental regimes envisaged by Jessica T. Mathews, as "a rolling process of intermediate or self-adjusting agreements that respond quickly to growing scientific understanding."[274] Even though open-ended commitments of this kind are still viewed with apprehension by diplomats, the "feedback loop" seems well on its way to becoming an established instrument of international environmental law—with a new obligation emerging for governments to take part in a deliberate, pre-programmed process of institutional learning.

Peter H. Sand is Senior Environmental Affairs Officer, United Nations Economic Commission for Europe (UN/ECE), Geneva. Views and opinions expressed in this paper are those of the author and do not necessarily reflect those of UN/ECE.

Notes

1. J. Jouzel et al., "Vostok Ice Core: A Continuous Isotope Temperature Record Over the Last Climatic Cycle (160,000 Years)"; J.M. Barnola et al., "Vostok Ice Core Provides 160,000-Year Record of Atmospheric CO_2"; C. Genthon et al., "Vostok Ice Core: Climatic Response to CO_2 and Orbital Forcing Changes Over the Last Climatic Cycle"; *Nature*, vol. 329 No. 6138 (1 October 1987) pp. 403–418. *See also* U. Siegenthaler & H. Oeschger, "Biospheric CO_2 Emissions During the Past 200 Years Reconstructed by Deconvolution of Ice Core Data," *Tellus*, vol. 39B (1987) pp. 140–154; D. Raynaud et al., "Climatic and CH_4 Cycle Implications of Glacial-Interglacial CH_4 Change in the Vostok Ice Core," *Nature*, vol. 333 No. 6174 (16 June 1988) pp. 655–657.

2. *See* T.F. Malone, "Mission to Planet Earth: Integrating Studies of Global Change," *Environment*, vol. 28 No. 8 (October 1986) pp. 6–9; and T.F. Malone & R. Correll, "Mission to Planet Earth Revisited: An Update on Studies of Global Change," *Environment*, vol. 31 No. 3 (April 1989) pp. 6–11, 31–35.

3. *Our Common Future*, World Commission on Environment and Development (Oxford 1987).

4. H. Cleveland, *The Future of International Governance* (Minneapolis 1986); N. Myers, "Environmental Challenges: More Government or Better Governance?," *Ambio*, vol. 17 No. 6 (1988) pp. 411–414.

5. *See*, for example, J. Schneider, *World Public Order of the Environment: Towards an International Ecological Law and Organization* (Toronto 1979); R. Boardman, *International Organization and the Conservation of Nature* (London 1981); G.P. Smith II, "The United Nations and the Environment: Sometimes a Great Notion?," *Texas International Law Journal*, vol. 19 (1984) pp. 335–364; and J. Eastby, *Functionalism and Interdependence* (Charlottesville/Va. 1985).

6. *See* E.B. Haas, "Why Collaborate? Issue-Linkage and International Regimes," *World Politics*, vol. 32 (1980) pp. 357–405, at pp. 358, 397; *International Regimes* (S.D. Krasner ed., Ithaca/N.Y. 1983); and W.J. Feld & R.S. Jordan, *International Organization* (2nd ed. New York 1988) pp. 243–277. On difficulties with regime definitions *see* S. Haggard & B.A. Simmons, "Theories of International Regimes," *International Organization*, vol. 41 (1987) pp. 491–517; and K.W. Abbott, "Modern International Relations Theory: A Prospectus for International Lawyers," *Yale Journal of International Law*, vol. 14 (1989) pp. 335–411, at pp. 338–339.

7. On the distinction see P.C. Jessup, *Transnational Law* (New Haven/Conn. 1956) p. 2.

8. One of the earliest comprehensive proposals to this effect was formulated in 1976 by

C. Tickell, *Climatic Change and World Affairs*, Harvard Studies in International Affairs No. 37 (Cambridge/Mass. 1977, reprinted Oxford 1978). While some of the points raised therein have since been answered in part by the 1977 UN *Convention on the Prohibition of Military or Any Other Hostile Use of Environmental Modification Techniques*, and by the 1980 UNEP *Provisions for Co-operation Between States in Weather Modification* (Governing Council Decision 8/7 A; *see* note 92 below), the proposal for a global framework convention reappears in a statement by Sir Crispin Tickell to the United Nations Economic and Social Council ("Global climate change," Statement by the Permanent Representative of the United Kingdom to the United Nations, New York, 8 May 1989). Possible elements for inclusion in a framework convention on climate change in the UNEP/WMO *Intergovernmental Panel on Climate Change* (IPCC) are summarized in the report of the second session of IPCC Working Group III, IPCC-III/Doc. 4 (1990) pp. 33–40.

9. For the Canadian and Maltese proposals, *see* J. Bruce, "Law of the Air: A Conceptual Outline," *Environmental Policy and Law*, vol. 18 (1988) p. 5; D.J. Attard, *Climate Change* (Malta 1989), pp. 11–18; and the statement by the International Meeting of Legal and Policy Experts on Protection of the Atmosphere (Ottawa, 22 February 1989).

10. Final Act, Convention and Annexes in U.N. Publication E.83.V.5 (New York 1983).

11. Term coined by A. Toffler, *Future Shock* (New York 1970) p. 124.

12. E.g., *see* M.O. Hudson, *International Legislation*, vol. 1 (Washington 1931) pp. XIII–LX; C. Eagleton, *International Government* (3rd ed., New York 1957) pp. 183–201; C.W. Jenks, *The Common Law of Mankind* (London 1958) pp. 183–184.

13. A.D. McNair, "The Functions and Differing Legal Character of Treaties," *British Yearbook of International Law*, vol. 11 (1930) pp. 100–118, at p. 101; reprinted in A.D. McNair, *The Law of Treaties* (rev. ed., Oxford 1961) pp. 739–740.

14. M. Olson, "Increasing the Incentives for International Cooperation," *International Organization*, vol. 25 (1971) pp. 866–874, at p. 874.

15. A. Underdal, *The Politics of International Fisheries Management: The Case of the Northeast Atlantic* (Oslo 1980) p. 36. I owe this reference to Edward L. Miles.

16. *See* in particular M. Olson, *The Logic of Collective Action: Public Goods and the Theory of Groups* (Cambridge/Mass., rev. ed. 1971) p. 51; and M. Olson, *The Rise and Decline of Nations* (New Haven/Conn. 1982) p. 21.

17. *International Legal Materials*, vol. 26 (1987) p. 1550. *See* P. Szell, "The Montreal Protocol on Substances That Deplete the Ozone Layer," *International Digest of Health Legislation*, vol. 39 (1988) pp. 278–282; W. Lang, "Diplomatie zwischen Oekonomie und Oekologie: das Beispiel des Ozonvertrags von Montreal," *Europa-Archiv*, vol. 43 (1988) pp. 105–110; J.G. Lammers, "Efforts to Develop a Protocol on Chlorofluorocarbons to the Vienna Convention for the Protection of the Ozone Layer," *Hague Yearbook of International Law*, vol. 1 (1988) pp. 225–269; G. Lean, *Action on Ozone* (Nairobi: UNEP 1989); and R.E. Benedick, *Ozone Diplomacy: New Directions in Safeguarding the Planet* (Washington, D.C. forthcoming, 1990).

18. E.g., *see* J. Erlichman, "Ozone Pact Full of Holes," *The Guardian* (London), 17 September 1987.

19. *United Nations Treaty Series*, vol. 1037, p. 151. *See* R.L. Meyer, "Travaux Preparatoires for the Unesco World Heritage Convention," *Earth Law Journal*, vol. 2 (1976) pp. 45–81; and S. Lyster, *International Wildlife Law* (Cambridge 1985) pp. 208–238.

20. World Heritage Committee (13th session, Paris, December 1989), Situation of the World Heritage Fund and Budget for 1990, Unesco Doc. SC–89/CONF.004/8 (1989).

21. E.g., *see* A.W. Koers, *International Regulation of Marine Fisheries: A Study of Regional Fisheries Organizations* (London 1973); and E. Hey, *The Regime for the Exploitation of Transboundary Marine Fisheries Resources* (Dordrecht 1989). On sealing, *see* Lyster (note 19 above), pp. 39–54.

22. *United Nations Treaty Series,* vol. 161 p. 72. *See* J. Scarff, "The International Management of Whales, Dolphins and Porpoises: An Interdisciplinary Assessment," *Ecology Law Quarterly,* vol. 6 (1977) pp. 343–352; S. Holt, "Whale Mining, Whale Saving," *Marine Policy,* vol. 9 (1985) pp. 192–213; and P.W. Birnie, *International Regulation of Whaling* (Dobbs Ferry/N.Y. 1985).

23. *International Legal Materials,* vol. 19 (1980) p. 841. *See* Lyster (note 19 above), pp. 156–177.

24. *International Legal Materials,* vol. 27 (1988) p. 868. *See* A.D. Watts, "The Convention on the Regulation of Antarctic Mineral Resource Activities," *International and Comparative Law Quarterly,* vol. 39 (1990) pp. 169–182; and for background, *The Antarctic Legal Regime* (C.C. Joyner & S.K. Chopra eds., Dordrecht 1988), and F. Orrego Vicuna, *Antarctic Mineral Exploitation: The Emerging Framework* (Cambridge 1988). On recent developments, *see* D.C. Waller, "Death of a Treaty: The Decline and Fall of the Antarctic Minerals Convention," *Vanderbilt Journal of Transnational Law,* vol. 22 (1989) pp. 631–668.

25. *United Nations Treaty Series,* vol. 993 p. 243. *See* D.S. Favre, *International Trade in Endangered Species: A Guide to CITES* (London 1989); J.C. Melick, "Regulation of International Trade in Endangered Wildlife," *Boston University International Law Journal,* vol.

1 (1982) pp. 249–275; A.H. Schonfeld, "International Trade in Wildlife: How Effective is the Endangered Species Treaty?," *California Western International Law Journal,* vol. 15 (1985) pp. 111–160; S. van Hoogstraten, "The Effectiveness of International Law With Regard to Endangered Species," *Yearbook of the Association of Attenders and Alumni of the Hague Academy of International Law,* vols. 54–56 (1986) pp. 157–168; and Lyster (note 19 above) pp. 239–277.

26. *See* the secretariat report to the seventh meeting of the Conference of the Parties (Lausanne, October 1989), "Operation of the Ivory Trade Control System," CITES Doc. 7.21 (1989); and M.J. Glennon, "Has International Law Failed the Elephant?," *American Journal of International Law,* vol. 84 (1990) pp. 1–43.

27. *United Nations Treaty Series,* vol. 729 p. 161. *See* M.I. Shaker, *The Nuclear Non-Proliferation Treaty: Origin and Implementation 1959–1979* (London 1980), vol. 1 pp. 300–470; and B.N. Schiff, *International Nuclear Technology Transfer: Dilemmas of Dissemination and Control* (Totowa/N.J. 1984).

28. Texts in P.H. Sand, *Marine Environment Law in the United Nations Environment Programme* (London 1988). *See* article 11(3) of the 1976 Barcelona Convention for the Protection of the Mediterranean Sea Against Pollution; article 10 of the 1980 Athens Protocol for the Protection of the Mediterranean Sea Against Pollution from Land-based Sources; article 13(3) of the 1983 Cartagena Convention for the Protection and Development of the Marine Environment of the Wider Caribbean Region; and article 18 of the 1986 Noumea Convention for the Protection of the Natural Resources and Environment of the South Pacific Region.

29. Article 4(2); *International Legal Materials,* vol. 26 (1987) p. 1529. For background *see* P. Szell, "The Vienna Convention for the

Protection of the Ozone Layer," *International Digest of Health Legislation*, vol. 36 (1985) pp. 839–842; P.H. Sand, "Protecting the Ozone Layer: The Vienna Convention Is Adopted," *Environment*, vol. 27 No. 5 (June 1985) pp. 18–43; W. Lang, "Luft und Ozon: Schutzobjekte des Völkerrechts," *Zeitschrift für ausländisches öffentliches Recht und Völkerrecht*, vol. 46 (1986) pp. 261–285; I. Rummel-Bulska, "Recent Developments Relating to the Vienna Convention for the Protection of the Ozone Layer," *Yearbook of the Association of Attenders and Alumni of the Hague Academy of International Law*, vol. 54/56 (1986) pp. 115–125; and M.K. Tolba, "The Ozone Agreement—and Beyond," *Environmental Conservation*, vol. 14 (1987) pp. 287–290.

30. Articles 10(2) and 14, *International Legal Materials*, vol. 28 (1989) p. 657. *See* A. Clerc, "The Basel Convention: Origins, Development and Potential Impact on Health and the Human Environment," *International Digest of Health Legislation*, vol. 40 (1989) pp. 903–907; F. Cotti, "Evolution of the Basel Convention," *Marine Policy*, vol. 14 (1990) pp. 210–213; S. Rublack, "Controlling Transboundary Movements of Hazardous Waste: The Evolution of a Global Convention," *Fletcher Forum of World Affairs*, vol. 13 (1989) pp. 113–125; S. Rublack, "Fighting Transboundary Waste Streams: Will the Basel Convention Help?," *Verfassung und Recht in Uebersee*, vol. 22 (1989) pp. 364–391; and M.K. Tolba, "The Global Agenda and the Hazardous Wastes Challenge," *Marine Policy*, vol. 14 (1990) pp. 205–209.

31. Open-ended Working Group of the Parties to the Montreal Protocol, Report of the Legal Drafting Group, U.N. Doc. UNEP/OzL.Pro.WG.II(1)/5 (November 1989), pp. 16–17; and the detailed cost estimates and financial proposals submitted to the second session of the second meeting, U.N. Docs. UNEP/OzL.Pro.WG.II(2)/3,4,5, 6 and 7 (March 1990). *See also* the report of the second session of the third meeting, UNEP/OzL.Pro.WG.III(2)/2 (May 1990).

32. Article 3 (Exchange of Technology), *International Legal Materials*, vol. 28 (1989) p. 214; *see* J.G. Lammers, "Second Report of the Committee on Legal Aspects of Long-Distance Air Pollution," *International Law Association: Report of the Warsaw Conference* (1988) pp. 5–8, 27–40; P.H. Sand, "Regional Approaches to Transboundary Air Pollution," in: *Energy: Production, Consumption, and Consequences* (J.L. Held ed., Washington 1990) pp. 246–264, at p. 255; and note 56 below.

33. For a progress report of the task force *see* Executive Body for the Convention on Long-range Transboundary Air Pollution, Report of the seventh session, U.N. Doc. ECE/EB.AIR/20 (1989) pp. 6–7.

34. Council Directive 88/609/EEC of 24 November 1988, *Official Journal of the European Communities*, No. L 336 (7 December 1988) p. 1. For background *see* Lammers (note 32 above) p. 16; and O. Lomas, "Environmental Protection, Economic Conflict and the European Community," *McGill Law Journal*, vol. 33 (1988) pp. 506–539, at p. 523.

35. *International Legal Materials*, vol. 16 (1977) p. 265. *See* A.C. Kiss, "The Protection of the Rhine Against Pollution," *Natural Resources Journal*, vol. 25 (1985) pp. 613–637; and J.G. Lammers, "The Rhine: Legal Aspects of the Management of a Transboundary River," in: *Nature Management and Sustainable Development* (W.D. Verwey ed., Amsterdam 1989) pp. 440–457. Further to a technical amendment in 1983 (text in Netherlands Tractatenblad 1983, No. 118), the convention was amended in December 1986 by way of a joint declaration of the heads of delegations to the *International Commission for the Protection of the Rhine against Pollution*.

36. U.N. General Assembly Resolution 2961/B (XXVII) adopted on 13 December 1972, amending "as a matter of principle" the scale of assessment which had originally set a maximum of 33.33 percent (Resolution

14/I of 13 February 1946), already reduced to 31.52 percent in 1957.

37. Article 1 (Definitions), note 32 above. *See* Lammers (note 32 above) pp. 42–43; *Critical Loads for Sulphur and Nitrogen* (J. Nilsson & P. Grennfelt eds.), Nordic Council of Ministers: Miljo Rapport No. 15 (Stockholm 1988); G. Persson, "Toward Resolution of the Acid Rain Controversy," in: *International Environmental Diplomacy* (J.E. Carroll ed., Cambridge 1988) pp. 189–196; and R.N. Mott, "Critical Loads Weighs In," *Environmental Forum*, vol. 6 No. 2 (1989) pp. 12–13.

38. *See* S. von Ciriacy-Wantrup, *Resource Conservation: Economics and Policies* (3rd ed., Berkeley 1968) pp. 251–258. To the extent that critical loads start from the concept of a finite "ecologically tolerable" level of pollution or other interference with an ecosystem, they may also be compared to the concepts of "carrying capacity" in range management or "environmental (receiving, assimilative, absorptive) capacity" in marine pollution management; *see* the definition in: *The State of the Marine Environment*, GESAMP Reports and Studies No. 39 (UNEP, Nairobi 1990) p. 82.

39. On the models developed for this purpose by the *International Institute for Applied Systems Analysis* (IIASA) *see* J. Alcamo, M. Amann, J.P. Hettelingh, M. Holmberg, L. Hordijk, J. Kamari, L. Kauppi, P. Kauppi, J. Kornai & A. Makela, "Acidification in Europe: A Simulation Model For Evaluating Control Strategies," *Ambio*, vol. 16 (1987) pp. 232–245; and L. Hordijk, "Linking Policy and Science: A Model Approach to Acid Rain," *Environment*, vol. 30 No. 2 (1988) pp. 17–20, 40–42.

40. On the importance of group size, *see* M. Olson (note 16 above) p. 21. "Regional" groups in this context do not have to be geographically contiguous, as illustrated by the non-contiguous OECD and EFTA groups.

41. *International Legal Materials,* vol. 13 (1974) pp. 352, 546. Regional cooperation in the North Sea had been initiated by the 1969 Bonn *Agreement for Cooperation in Dealing with Pollution of the North Sea by Oil* (extended to other harmful substances in 1983) and the 1972 Oslo *Convention for the Prevention of Marine Pollution from Ships and Aircraft*; texts in *United Nations Treaty Series*, vol. 704 p. 3, and *International Legal Materials*, vol. 11 (1972) p. 263. *See* J.A. de Yturriaga, "Regional Conventions on the Protection of the Marine Environment," *Recueil des Cours de l'Académie de Droit International*, vol. 162 (1979) pp. 319–449; D.L. Fluharty, *International Regulation of Access to and Use of Resources in the Baltic Sea*, Ph.D. thesis, University of Michigan (Ann Arbor 1977); *Comprehensive Security for the Baltic: An Environmental Approach* (A.H. Westing ed., Oslo 1989); the annual reports of the Baltic Marine Environment Protection Commission (HELCOM, 11th session: Helsinki, February 1990) and of the joint Oslo and Paris Commissions (OSPARCOM, 11th session: Dublin, June 1989); and the report of the *Third International Conference for the Protection of the North Sea* (The Hague, March 1990).

42. Final Act, Convention and Protocols in *International Legal Materials*, vol. 15 (1976) p. 290. *See* B. Boxer, "Mediterranen Pollution: Problem and Response," *Ocean Development and International Law*, vol. 10 (1982) pp. 315–356; and P.M. Haas, *Saving the Mediterranean: The Politics of International Environmental Cooperation* (New York 1990).

43. *See* D.M. Johnston & L.M.G. Enomoto, "Regional Approaches to the Protection and Conservation of the Marine Environment," in: *The Environmental Law of the Sea* (D.M. Johnston ed., Gland/Switzerland 1981) pp. 285–385; B.A. Boczek, "Global and Regional Approaches to the Protection and Preservation of the Marine Environment," *Case Western Reserve Journal of International Law*, vol. 16 (1984) pp. 39–70; and

D. Edwards, "Review of the Status of Implementation and Development of Regional Arrangements on Cooperation in Combating Marine Pollution," in: *International Environmental Diplomacy* (J.E. Carroll ed., Cambridge 1988) pp. 229–272.

44. Texts and membership lists in P.H. Sand, *Marine Environment Law in the United Nations Environment Programme* (London 1988).

45. Ibid., pp. 226, 235. *See* D.M. Johnston, "Systemic Environmental Damage: The Challenge to International Law and Organization," *Syracuse Journal of International Law and Commerce*, vol. 12 (1985) pp. 255–282; and Qing-Nan Meng, *Land-Based Marine Pollution: International Law Development* (London 1987).

46. *See* the progress reports to the UNEP Governing Council, Doc. UNEP/GC.13/9/Add.1 (1984) and UNEP/GC.15/9/Add.2 (1989).

47. Texts in Sand (note 44 above) pp. 27, 103. *See* S. Kuwabara, *The Legal Regime of the Protection of the Mediterranean against Pollution from Land-Based Sources* (Dublin 1984). For example, emission standards for mercury were adopted under the Athens Protocol in 1987, text in *Medwaves* No. 10/III (1987) p. 4; limit values and water quality objectives for cadmium compounds and for DDT levels in 1989, *Medwaves* No. 18/III-IV (1989) pp. 3–6.

48. Signed on 29 March 1989 under the auspices of the UNEP-sponsored *Regional Organization for the Protection of the Marine Environment* (ROPME), pursuant to the 1978 Kuwait Regional Convention for Cooperation on the Protection of the Marine Environment from Pollution; *United Nations Treaty Series*, vol. 1140 p. 133. For a summary of ongoing cooperation, for instance on the occasion of oilspills as a result of military attacks on offshore platforms during the Iran-Iraq war, *see* M. Gerges, "Satellite in Action in ROPME Sea Area," *Siren* No. 40 (March 1989) pp. 23–26.

49. *See* Transfrontier Movements of Hazardous Wastes: Proceedings of a Seminar on Legal and Institutional Aspects of Transfrontier Movements held in Paris 12–14 June 1984 (Paris, OECD 1985); and the report by the OECD Waste Management Policy Group, Monitoring and Control of Transfrontier Movements of Hazardous Wastes: OECD Activities 1983–1989, OECD Doc. ENV/WMP/89.4 (September 1989).

50. *See* Greenpeace International, *International Trade in Toxic Wastes: Policy and Data Analysis* (2nd ed. London 1988); and the periodical *Greenpeace Waste Trade Update* (vols. 1–3, Washington 1988–1990).

51. Note 30 above; *see* OECD Council Resolutions C(89)1 of 30 January 1989 and C(89)112 of 20 July 1989, in OECD Doc. ENV/WMP/89.4 (note 49 above), Appendix 1.

52. OAU Resolution CM/RES. 1225 (L) of 21 July 1989.

53. Revision of Council Directives 84/631/EEC (intra-Community shipments) and 86/279/EEC (exports from the Community), announced on 4 October 1989, *International Environment Reporter*, vol. 12 No. 11 (8 November 1989) p. 531; on the previous regime *see* M.E. Kelly, "International Regulation of Transfrontier Hazardous Waste Shipments: A New EEC Environmental Directive," *Texas International Law Journal*, vol. 21 (1985) pp. 977–996. The EEC has also agreed to ban all hazardous and radioactive waste exports to the 69 developing countries participating in the ACP-EEC ("Lome IV") Convention signed on 15 December 1989; *see* C. Cova, "Lome IV: une convention pour 10 ans," *Revue du Marché Commun*, No. 333 (1990) pp. 1–2.

54. Text in *Selected Multilateral Treaties in the Field of the Environment*, UNEP Reference

Series No. 3 (A.C. Kiss ed., Nairobi 1983) p. 214; amendment protocol of 25 October 1983 in *International Environmental Law: Multilateral Treaties*, vol. 5 (W.E. Burhenne ed., Berlin 1985) p. 968:69/A/1.

55. Council Directive 73/404/EEC of 22 November 1973 on the Approximation of the Laws of the Member States relating to Detergents, *Official Journal of the European Communities* No. L 347 (17 December 1973) p. 51, as amended by Directive 86/94/EEC.

56. *International Legal Materials*, vol. 18 (1979) p. 1442. For background *see* G.S. Wetstone & A. Rosencranz, *Acid Rain in Europe and North America: National Responses to an International Problem* (Washington 1983); E.M. Chossudovsky, *"East-West" Diplomacy for Environment in the United Nations*, UNITAR Study E.88/XV/ST26 (Geneva 1989); A. Fraenkel, "The Convention on Long-range Transboundary Air Pollution: Meeting the Challenge of International Cooperation," *Harvard International Law Journal*, vol. 30 (1989) pp. 447–476; and Sand (note 32 above).

57. Declaration adopted by the International Conference of Ministers on Acid Rain, Ottawa, 21 March 1984, text in *Netherlands Tractatenblad* (1984) No. 57; and governmental statements made at the Multilateral Conference on the Environment, Munich, 27 June 1984. *See* J. McCormick, *Acid Earth: The Global Threat of Acid Pollution* (London 1985) pp. 64–68; and L. Gundling, "Multilateral Cooperation of States under the ECE Convention on Long-Range Transboundary Air Pollution," in: *Transboundary Air Pollution: International Legal Aspects of the Cooperation of States* (C. Flinterman, B. Kwiatkowska & J.G. Lammers eds., Dordrecht 1986) pp. 19–31.

58. *International Legal Materials*, vol. 27 (1988) p. 707. *See* H. Vygen, "Air Pollution Control: Success of East-West Cooperation," *Environmental Policy and Law*, vol. 15 (1985) pp.

6–8; and L. Bjorkbom, "Resolution of Environmental Problems: The Use of Diplomacy," in: *International Environmental Diplomacy* (J.E. Carroll ed., Cambridge 1988) pp. 123–137.

59. Note on draft article 2, Working Group on Nitrogen Oxides, Report of the sixth session, U.N. Doc. EB.AIR/WG.3/12, Annex I, p. 3 (September 1987), reprinted in *Environmental Policy and Law*, vol. 17 (1987) p. 259. *See* Lammers (note 32 above) p. 6; R.N. Mott, "Nitrogen Oxides," *Environmental Policy and Law*, vol. 18 (1988) pp. 52–53; and R.N. Mott, "An Acid Rain Summons From Europe," *Environmental Forum*, vol. 5 No. 1 (1988) pp. 32–33.

60. *International Legal Materials*, vol. 28 (1989) p. 214. *See* Fraenkel (note 56 above) pp. 472–475.

61. Declaration on the 30-percent Reduction of Nitrogen Oxide Emissions, 31 October 1988; text in *Environmental Policy and Law*, vol. 18 (1988) p. 234. *See* Sand (note 32 above) p. 255.

62. *See* the country-by-country tables of overachievement pledges in *Ambio*, vol. 15 (1986) p. 48; and in *Acid Magazine*, No. 8 (1989) pp. 5–6.

63. United Nations Economic Commission for Europe, *The State of Transboundary Air Pollution*, Air Pollution Studies No. 5, U.N. Doc. E.89.II.E.25 (New York 1989) p. 14. For a table of actual emission reductions between 1980 and 1986 (16.4 percent for Europe as a whole), *see* T. Iversen, "Some Recent Developments at the Meteorological Synthesizing Centre West (MS-W) of EMEP," *MonitAir* No. 3 (1989) pp. 2–11, at p. 4.

64. Note 17 above; and Lammers (note 32 above) pp. 8–14.

65. Commission of the European Communities, *The Week in Europe*, WE/9/89 (9 March 1989).

More recently, the EEC Commission has proposed to accelerate the schedule further, so as to phase out production of CFCs by 1997 and of halons by 1998; *see* M. Jachtenfuss, ''The European Community and the Protection of the Ozone Layer,'' *Journal of Common Market Studies*, vol. 28 (1990) pp. 261–277, at p. 271.

66. Helsinki Declaration on the Protection of the Ozone Layer, U.N. Doc. UNEP/OzL.Pro.1/5, Appendix I; *International Legal Materials*, vol. 28 (1989) p. 1335.

67. *See* the summary by Lean (note 17 above) pp. 8–10.

68. *United Nations Treaty Series*, vol. 55 p. 194.

69. GATT Standards Code (in force since 1 January 1980), article 2.2: ''Where technical regulations or standards are required and relevant international standards exist or their completion is imminent, Parties shall use them, or the relevant parts of them, as a basis for the technical regulations or standards except where, as duly explained upon request, such international standards or relevant parts are inappropriate for the Parties concerned, for inter alia such reasons as national security requirements; the prevention of deceptive practices; protection for human health or safety, animal or plant life or health, or the environment; fundamental climatic or geographical factors; fundamental technological problems.''

70. Article 601, in *International Legal Materials*, vol. 27 (1988) p. 281; *see also* the cross-reference to GATT in article 1201 of the agreement.

71. In this context, the EEC Commission has initiated infringement proceedings under article 169 of the Treaty against Denmark, the Federal Republic of Germany, Greece and the Netherlands. On the dispute with Denmark *see* Lomas (note 34 above) p. 531; on the disputes over car emission standards *see* K. Hailbronner, ''Der 'nationale Alleingang' im Gemeinschaftsrecht am Beispiel der Abgasstandards für PKW,'' *Europäische Grundrechts-Zeitschrift*, vol. 16 (1989) pp. 101–122.

72. *International Legal Materials*, vol. 25 (1986) p. 506. *See* G.A. Bermann, ''The Single European Act: A New Constitution for the Community?,'' *Columbia Journal of Transnational Law*, vol. 27 (1989) pp. 529–587.

73. *See* Bermann (note 72 above) pp. 543–545, 558–561; and D.H. Scheuing, ''Umweltschutz auf der Grundlage der Einheitlichen Europäischen Akte,'' *Europarecht*, vol. 24 (1989) pp. 152–192.

74. *Toward Wider Acceptance of U.N. Treaties* (UNITAR, New York 1971) pp. 34–40. *See also* R. Churchill, ''Why Do Marine Pollution Conventions Take So Long To Enter Into Force?,'' *Maritime Policy and Management*, vol. 4 (1976) pp. 41–49.

75. Note 66 above. According to article 9(5) of the Vienna Convention (note 29 above), any textual amendment of the Montreal Protocol (note 17 above) must be ratified by at least two-thirds of the Parties (i.e., currently 37 out of 55) to become legally binding—which is likely to take a minimum of two years after the amendment conference scheduled to be held in London in June 1990. By contrast, had the reduction rates been laid down in an annex to the Protocol, their amendment would become effective six months after communication to the Parties (article 10/2/c of the Vienna Convention).

76. Article 25 (*United Nations Treaty Series*, vol. 1155 p. 331): ''A treaty or part of a treaty is applied provisionally pending its entry into force if (a) the treaty itself so provides; or (b) the negotiating states have in some other manner so agreed.''

77. *United Nations Treaty Series*, vol. 55 p. 308. *See* J.H. Jackson, *World Trade and the Law of*

GATT (Indianapolis 1969) pp. 60–63; F. Roessler, "The Provisional Application of the GATT," *Journal of World Trade Law*, vol. 19 (1985) pp. 289–295; and M. Hansen & E. Vermulst, "The GATT Protocol of Provisional Application: A Dying Grandfather?," *Columbia Journal of Transnational Law*, vol. 27 (1989) pp. 263–308.

78. Note 56 above.

79. "Resolution on Long-range Transboundary Air Pollution," in: Economic Commission for Europe, Report of the high-level meeting within the framework of the ECE on the protection of the environment, U.N. Doc. ECE/HLM.1/2, vol. I Annex II (1980).

80. *See* Chossudovsky (note 56 above) pp. 122–141.

81. *International Legal Materials*, vol. 24 (1985) p. 484.

82. "Resolution on Long-term Financing of the Co-operative Programme for Monitoring and Evaluation of the Long-range Transmission of Air Pollutants in Europe (EMEP)," in: Executive Body for the Convention on Long-range Transboundary Air Pollution, Report of the second session, U.N. Doc. ECE/EB.AIR/4, Annex III (1984).

83. *See* UN/ECE, "EMEP: The Co-operative Programme for Monitoring and Evaluation of the Long-range Transmission of Air Pollutants in Europe," *Economic Bulletin for Europe*, vol. 34 No. 1 (1982) pp. 29–40; "The Third Phase of EMEP: 1984–1986," in: *The State of Transboundary Air Pollution* (note 63 above) pp. 19–38; H. Dovland, "Monitoring European Transboundary Air Pollution," *Environment*, vol. 29 No. 10 (1987) pp. 10–15, 27–28; and T. Iversen (note 63 above).

84. Note 30 above.

85. Resolution No. 4 ("Responsibility of States for the Implementation of the Basel Convention on the Control of Transboundary Movements of Hazardous Wastes and their Disposal"), adopted on 22 March 1989.

86. *See* C.M. Chinkin, "The Challenge of Soft Law: Development and Change in International Law," *International and Comparative Law Quarterly*, vol. 38 (1989) pp. 850–866; and for application of the concept to the environment, e.g., A.C. Kiss, *Survey of Current Developments in International Environmental Law*, IUCN Environmental Policy and Law Paper No. 10 (Morges/Switzerland 1976) p. 23.

87. Note 61 above.

88. *Der Spiegel*, No. 5 (30 January 1989) p. 94.

89. P.H. Sand, "Environmental Law in the United Nations Environment Programme," in: *The Future of the International Law of the Environment* (R.J. Dupuy ed., Dordrecht 1985) pp. 51–88, at pp. 56–60.

90. U.N. General Assembly Resolution 37/7 of 28 October 1982. *See* W.E. Burhenne & W.A. Irwin, *The World Charter for Nature: A Background Paper* (Berlin 1983); and H.W. Wood Jr., "The United Nations World Charter for Nature: the Developing Nations' Initiative to Establish Protections for the Environment," *Ecology Law Quarterly*, vol. 12 (1985) pp. 977–996.

91. U.N. General Assembly Resolution 37/217 of 20 December 1982; text of the conclusions in Sand (note 44 above) p. 226.

92. UNEP Governing Council Decision 8/7/A of 29 April 1980.

93. UNEP Governing Council Decision 6/14 of 19 May 1978. *See* A.O. Adede, "United Nations Efforts Toward the Development of an Environmental Code of Conduct for States Concerning Harmonious Utilization of Shared Natural Resources," *Albany Law Review*, vol. 43 (1979) pp. 488–519; J.A. Barberis, *Los*

45

recursos naturales compartidos entre estados y el derecho internacional (Madrid 1979) pp. 147–165; and W. Riphagen, "The International Concern For the Environment As Expressed in the Concept of the 'Common Heritage of Mankind' and of 'Shared Natural Resources'," in: *Trends in Environmental Policy and Law*, IUCN Environmental Policy and Law Paper No. 15 (M. Bothe ed., Gland/Switzerland 1980) pp. 343–362.

94. *See* the progress report to the UNEP Governing Council, U.N. Doc. UNEP/GC.13/9/Add.1 (1984) p. 7.

95. UNEP Governing Council Decision 14/30 of 17 June 1987.

96. Note 30 above.

97. UNEP Governing Council Decision 12/14 of 28 May 1984; *see also* note 204 below.

98. International Law Association, *Report of the Fifty-second Conference in Helsinki* 1966 (London 1967) pp. 484–532.

99. Note 3 above. *See also* the commentary, Environmental Protection and Sustainable Development: Legal Principles and Recommendations adopted by the Experts Group on Environmental Law of the World Commission on Environment and Development (London 1986).

100. World Health Organization, *Guidelines for Drinking-Water Quality*, vols. 1–3 (Geneva 1984–1985); *see* Setting Environmental Standards: Guidelines for Decision-Making (H.W. de Koning ed., WHO Geneva 1987) p. 10 and Annex 6.

101. E.g., "Oxides of Nitrogen," "Photochemical Oxidants," and "Sulphur Oxides and Suspended Particulate Matter," WHO Environmental Health Criteria Documents No. 4, 7 and 8 (Geneva 1977–1979); and "Air Quality Guidelines for Europe,"

WHO Regional Publications: European Series No. 23 (Copenhagen 1987).

102. *See* World Resources Institute, *World Resources 1988–89* (New York 1988) pp. 333, 345; United Nations Environment Programme, *Environmental Data Report 1989–90* (Oxford 1989) p. 13; H. French, *Clearing the Air: A Global Agenda*, Worldwatch Paper No. 94 (Washington 1990) p. 9–16; all of which refer to "WHO air quality standards."

103. Uniform standards are prepared by technical expert committees (e.g., for ambient air quality measurement by ISO Technical Committee 146), circulated to all member bodies for voting by correspondence, and if 75 percent of the votes cast are in favor, published by the ISO Council as accepted international standards. *See* L.C. Verman, *Standardization: A New Discipline* (Hamden/Conn. 1973); and International Electrotechnical Commission & International Organization for Standardization, *Directives: Procedures for the Technical Work*, Part 1 (1st ed. Geneva 1989) pp. 14–23.

104. Article 13 of the International Telegraphic Convention, signed at St. Petersburg in 1875; *American Journal of International Law*, Supplement vol. 7 (1913) p. 276. The method of "technical" adjustments proved so effective that the convention did not require diplomatic revision until 1932, when it was combined with the Radiotelegraphic Convention into the present ITU Convention. *See* G.A. Codding, *The International Telecommunication Union: An Experiment in International Co-operation* (Leyden 1952) p. 28; and E. Yemin, *Legislative Powers in the United Nations and Specialized Agencies* (Leyden 1969) pp. 63–84.

105. Article 13 of the Treaty Concerning the Formation of a General Postal Union, signed at Bern in 1874. *See* G.A. Codding, *The Universal Postal Union* (New York 1964) p. 107; and Yemin (note 104 above) pp. 85–113.

106. From article 60(2) of the 1924 Bern Conventions concerning the Transport of Goods by Rail (CIM) and concerning the Transport of Passengers and Luggage by Rail (CIV) (*League of Nations Treaty Series*, vol. 77 p. 367 and vol. 78 p. 17) to article 14(3) of the 1957 UN/ECE European Agreement concerning the International Carriage of Dangerous Goods by Road (ADR), *United Nations Treaty Series* vol. 619 p. 79 (with technical annexes as amended through 1990, U.N. Doc. E.89.VIII.2, 2 vols.).

107. Adopted under article 21 of the 1946 WHO Constitution, *United Nations Treaty Series*, vol. 14 p. 185. *See* H.B. Jacobini, ''The New International Sanitary Regulations,'' *American Journal of International Law*, vol. 46 (1952) pp. 727–728; Yemin (note 104 above) pp. 181–205; and D.M. Leive, *International Regulatory Regimes: Case Studies in Health, Meteorology, and Food*, vol. I (Lexington/Mass. 1976) pp. 3–152.

108. Adopted under articles 7(d) and 10(b) of the 1947 WMO Constitution; *United Nations Treaty Series*, vol. 77 p. 143. *See* I. Detter, *Law Making by International Organizations* (Stockholm 1965) pp. 228–234; Yemin (note 104 above) pp. 161–180; and Leive (note 107 above) pp. 232–326.

109. Adopted under article 7 of the 1965 Convention on Facilitation of International Maritime Traffic; *United Nations Treaty Series*, vol. 591 p. 265. *See* C.H. Alexandrowicz, ''The Convention on Facilitation of International Maritime Traffic and International Technical Regulation: A Comparative Study,'' *International and Comparative Law Quarterly*, vol. 15 (1966) pp. 621–638. On the influence of ICAO practice (notes 119–126 below) *see* J. Erler, ''Regulatory Procedures of ICAO as a Model for IMCO,'' *McGill Law Journal*, vol. 10 (1964) pp. 262–268; and C.H. Alexandrowicz, *The Law-Making Functions of the Specialized Agencies of the United Nations* (Sydney 1973). On efforts to cope with the problem of ratification delays in subsequent IMO conventions on marine pollution (note 141 below), *see* A.B. Sielen & R.J. McManus, ''IMCO and the Politics of Ship Pollution,'' in: D.A. Kay & H. Jacobsen, *Environmental Protection: The International Dimension* (Totowa/N.J. 1983) pp. 140–183, at pp. 152–153, 172–174.

110. *See* J.P. Dobbert, ''Decisions of International Organizations—Effectiveness in Member States: Some Aspects of the Law and Practice of FAO,'' in: *The Effectiveness of International Decisions* (S.M. Schwebel ed., Leyden 1971) pp. 206–276, at pp. 238–256; and Leive (note 107 above), vol. II pp. 375–541.

111. P. Contini & P.H. Sand, ''Methods to Expedite Environment Protection: International Ecostandards,'' *American Journal of International Law*, vol. 66 (1972) pp. 37–59 (originally submitted as a preparatory document for the U.N. Conference on the Human Environment, A/CONF.48/PC.II/CRP.3, February 1971); and P.H. Sand, ''The Creation of Transnational Rules for Environmental Protection,'' in: *Trends in Environmental Policy and Law*, IUCN Environmental Policy and Law Paper No. 15 (M. Bothe ed., Gland/Switzerland 1980) pp. 311–320.

112. E.g., *see* J.H. Cumberland, ''The Role of Uniform Standards in International Environmental Management,'' in: *Problems of Environmental Economics* (OECD, Paris 1972) pp. 239–253; M. Bothe, ''The Trends in Both National and International Politics for Achieving a Unification of Standards in Pollution Matters,'' *Zeitschrift für Umweltpolitik*, vol. 2 (1979) pp. 293–312; V. Vukasovic, ''Ekoloski standardi i razvoj'' [Ecological Standards and Development], *Medunarodni Problemi*, vol. 35 (1983) pp. 47–58; A.M. Abdelhady, ''Nécessité d'établir des normes uniformes relatives à l'environnement,'' *Revue Egyptienne de*

Droit International, vol. 41 (1985) pp. 1–28; and P.M. Dupuy, "Le droit international de l'environnement et la souveraineté des Etats: bilan et perspective," in: *The Future of the International Law of the Environment* (R.J. Dupuy ed., Dordrecht 1985) pp. 29–50, at pp. 35–37. On regional harmonization of environmental standards in the European Community, *see* E. Rehbinder & R. Stewart, "Legal Integration in Federal Systems: European Community Environmental Law," *American Journal of Comparative Law*, vol. 33 (1985) pp. 371–446.

113. *See* the list in Contini & Sand (note 111 above, p. 55 n. 117), which includes health standards (note 107 above), food quality standards (note 110 above), conservation standards for protected areas (note 19 above) and marine living resources (notes 21–23 above), radiation protection standards (under article 3 of the Statute of the International Atomic Energy Agency; *United Nations Treaty Series*, vol. 276 p. 3), aircraft emission standards (note 120 below), etc.

114. Under article 24 of the 1974 Helsinki Convention (note 41 above) and article 17 of the 1976 Barcelona Convention (notes 42 and 47 above). On the mutual influence of these two conventions during their drafting stage, *see* P.H. Sand, "The Rise of Regional Agreements for Marine Environment Protection," in: *The Law and the Sea: Essays in Memory of Jean Carroz* (FAO, Rome 1987) pp. 223–232, at p. 329 n. 3; reprinted in *International Digest of Health Legislation*, vol. 39 (1988) pp. 499–513.

115. K. Kaiser, "Transnational Relations as a Threat to the Democratic Process," *International Organization*, vol. 25 (1971) pp. 706–720.

116. In response to a 1983 resolution, the EEC Commission now submits annual reports to Parliament on the application of Community law. The sixth report (for the year 1988) was published in the *Official Journal of the European Communities*, No. C 330 (30 December 1989) pp. 1–160; for a summary of the section on environmental law, *see Europe Environment* No. 335 (31 January 1990), Document Features pp. 1–10. On the increased powers of the European Parliament under the 1986 Single European Act, *see* Bermann (note 72 above) pp. 575–583; D.S. Lew, "The EEC Legislative Process: An Evolving Balance," *Columbia Journal of Transnational Law*, vol. 27 (1989) pp. 679–719; and for the environmental implications, Scheuing (note 73 above).

117. *See* Dobbert (note 110 above) pp. 250–256; and Leive (note 107 above) vol. II pp. 461–484.

118. *See* Contini & Sand (note 111 above) pp. 49–52. Opting out or "contracting out" has been practised by international organizations for more than a century, and actually goes back to the 1874 Bern Treaty establishing the Universal Postal Union (note 105 above); *see* G.A. Codding Jr., "Contributions of the World Health Organization and the International Civil Aviation Organization to the Development of International Law," *Proceedings of the American Society of International Law*, vol. 59 (1965) pp. 147–153, at p. 152.

119. *United Nations Treaty Series*, vol. 15 p. 295. *See* T. Buergenthal, *Law-Making in the International Civil Aviation Organization* (Syracuse/N.Y. 1969) pp. 76–101. The simplified amendment procedure goes back to the "technical regulations" under article 34 of the 1919 Paris Convention on the Regulation of Air Navigation (*League of Nations Treaty Series*, vol. 11 p. 173), which via article 61 of the 1933 International Sanitary Convention for Aerial Navigation (*League of Nations Treaty Series*, vol. 161 p. 65) in turn became the model for the WHO international health regulations (note 107 above).

120. ICAO, "International Standards and Recommended Practices on Environmental Protection," Annex 16 to the Convention on International Civil Aviation, vol. II: Aircraft Engine Emissions (1st ed. 1981, as amended by the Council on 4 March 1988). Vol. I of Annex 16 (1st ed. 1971, 2nd ed. 1988) deals with aircraft noise standards; *see* R. Goy, "La lutte de l'OACI contre le bruit des aéronefs," *Environmental Policy and Law*, vol. 2 (1976) pp. 72–76; and for stricter EEC standards, Council Directive 89/629, *Official Journal of the European Communities*, No. L 363 (13 December 1989) p. 27.

121. According to a proposal for amendment of article 50(a), introduced at the 27th ICAO Assembly in 1989 for submission to an extraordinary assembly in 1990, the number of Council members is expected to be increased to 36.

122. Pursuant to a 1947 decision of the ICAO Assembly; *see* R.H. Mankiewicz, "Organisation de l'aviation civile internationale," *Annuaire français de droit international*, vol. 2 (1956) pp. 643–666, at p. 650.

123. Article 90.

124. Article 38.

125. Article 12; *see* J.E. Carroz, "International Legislation on Air Navigation Over the High Seas," *Journal of Air Law and Commerce*, vol. 26 (1959) pp. 158–172.

126. When the membership of the 1919 Paris Convention (note 119 above) was expanded in the 1930s to include a number of developing countries, it became apparent that many of these were technologically unable to comply with some advanced international aviation standards and consequently had to be given an option to follow their own standards, provided due notice was given to this effect. Gradually, this practice developed into a flexible system of "notification of national departures" from worldwide standards, eventually codified in present article 38 of the 1944 Chicago Convention, which Buergenthal (note 119 above, p. 221) labels "real genius"; *see also* F.C. Thayer, "International Air Transport: A Microsystem in Need of New Approaches," *International Organization*, vol. 25 (1971) pp. 875–898, at p. 884.

127. K. Skubiszewski, "Enactment of Law by International Organizations," *British Yearbook of International Law*, vol. 41 (1968) pp. 198–274, at p. 273; *see also* K. Skubiszewski, "Forms of Participation of International Organizations in the Lawmaking Process," *International Organization*, vol. 18 (1964) pp. 790–805.

128. D.W. Bowett, *The Law of International Institutions* (4th ed., London 1982) p. 146.

129. *International Legal Materials*, vol. 28 (1989) p. 1308; *see* P.J. Sands, "The Environment, Community and International Law," *Harvard International Law Journal*, vol. 30 (1989) pp. 393–420.

130. G. Scelle, *Précis de droit des gens*, Pt. I (Paris 1932) p. 43.

131. Case concerning military and paramilitary activities in and against Nicaragua *(Nicaragua v. United States)*, judgment of 26 November 1984 with regard to jurisdiction of the court and admissibility of the application, *International Legal Materials*, vol. 24 (1985) p. 59. *See also* the statement of 18 January 1985 on United States withdrawal from the proceedings initiated by Nicaragua in the International Court of Justice, with observations by the U.S. State Department, *International Legal Materials*, vol. 24 (1985) pp. 246, 249; and the comments in *American Journal of International Law*, vol. 79 No. 2 (1985). For a succinct summary *see* M. Akehurst, "Nicaragua v. United States of America," *Indian Journal of International Law*, vol. 27 (1987) pp. 357–384.

132. Article 23; *International Legal Materials*, vol. 22 (1983) p. 221. *See* N.B. Frazer & M.J. Peterson, ''Protecting Caribbean Waters: the Cartagena Convention,'' *Oceanus*, vol. 27 No. 3 (1984) pp. 85–88; and G. Bundschuh, ''Transfrontier Pollution: Convention for the Protection and Development of the Marine Environment of the Wider Caribbean: Agreement Involving Collective Response to Marine Pollution Incidents and Long Range Environmental Planning,'' *Georgia Journal of International and Comparative Law*, vol. 14 (1984) pp. 201–215.

133. U.N. Doc. UNEP/IG.53/5/Rev.1 (1985), appended to the Final Act of the Vienna Conference of Plenipotentiaries on the Protection of the Ozone Layer, paragraph 1: ''The delegations of Australia, Austria, Belgium, Canada, Chile, Denmark, Finland, France, Germany (Federal Republic of), Italy, Netherlands, New Zealand, Norway, Sweden, Switzerland, and United Kingdom of Great Britain and Northern Ireland express their regret at the absence from the Vienna Convention for the Protection of the Ozone Layer of any provision for the compulsory settlement of disputes by third parties, at the request of one party. Consistently with their traditional support for such a procedure, these delegations appeal to all Parties to the Convention to make use of the possibility of a declaration under article 11, paragraph 3, of the Convention.''

134. Article 11 (note 29 above). This provision also applies to the 1987 Montreal Protocol (note 17 above), pursuant to article 14 of the latter.

135. Article 20 (note 30 above).

136. Declaration of 7 April 1970, excluding from the compulsory jurisdiction of the International Court of Justice ''disputes arising out of or concerning jurisdiction or rights claimed or exercised by Canada in respect of the conservation, management and exploitation of the living resources of the sea, or in respect of the prevention or control of pollution or contamination of the marine environment in marine areas adjacent to the coast of Canada''; *International Legal Materials*, vol. 9 (1970) p. 598. The declaration was withdrawn on 10 September 1985; *see International Legal Materials*, vol. 24 (1985) p. 1729.

137. *See* the proposal for special environmental chambers of the court, by Judge Philip C. Jessup, ''Do New Problems Need New Courts?,'' *Proceedings of the American Society of International Law*, vol. 65 (1971) pp. 261–268; reiterated by Judge Manfred Lachs, ''Some Reflections on the Settlement of International Disputes,'' *Proceedings of the American Society of International Law*, vol. 68 (1974) pp. 323–330, at p. 328; and the proposal for a new ''world tribunal to enforce proper regulation in environmental matters,'' by the late Judge Nagendra Singh, ''The environmental law of war and the future of mankind,'' in: *The Future of the International Law of the Environment* (R.J. Dupuy ed., Dordrecht 1985) pp. 419–423, at p. 422.

138. *See* the statistical survey of dispute settlement clauses in multilateral environmental agreements, by A.C. Kiss, ''Le règlement des différends dans les conventions multilaterales relatives à la protection de l'environnement,'' in: *The Settlement of Disputes on the New Natural Resources* (R.J. Dupuy ed., The Hague 1983) pp. 119–130.

139. E.g., *see* K. Sachariew, ''State Responsibility for Multilateral Treaty Violations: Identifiying the 'Injured State' and Its Legal Status,'' *Netherlands International Law Review*, vol. 35 (1988) pp. 273–289.

140. *See* note 214 below.

141. Note 107 above.

142. *United Nations Treaty Series*, vol. 150 p. 67, with the supplementary Plant Protection Agreement for South East Asia and the Pacific Region (*United Nations Treaty Series*, vol. 247 p. 400); *see* Dobbert (note 110 above) pp. 217–221.

143. *International Legal Materials*, vol. 12 (1973) p. 1319, and vol. 17 (1978) p. 546. *See* R.M. M'Gonigle & M.W. Zacher, *Pollution, Politics and International Law: Tankers at Sea* (Berkeley 1979); and G.J. Timagenis, *International Control of Marine Pollution*, 2 vols. (Dobbs Ferry/N.Y. 1980). For the revised model certificate *see* the IMO Regulations for the Prevention of Pollution by Oil (London 1982) p. 119.

144. *United Nations Treaty Series*, vol. 1046 p. 120. And *see* the 1972 Oslo Convention (note 41 above), the 1976 Barcelona Protocol for the Prevention of Pollution of the Mediterranean Sea by Dumping from Ships and Aircraft (note 42 above), the 1976 Bonn Convention for the Protection of the Rhine against Chemical Pollution (*International Legal Materials*, vol. 16, 1977, p. 242), EEC Directive 76/464 on Pollution Caused by Certain Dangerous Substances Discharged into the Aquatic Environment of the Community (*Official Journal of the European Communities*, No. L 129 of 18 May 1976, as amended to 1988), EEC Directive 80/68 on the Protection of Groundwater against Pollution Caused by Dangerous Substances (*Official Journal of the European Communities*, No. L 20 of 26 January 1980); etc.

145. Note 30 above.

146. World Health Assembly Resolution 28.65; *WHO Official Acts* No. 226, Annex 12 (1975). *See* D.A. Kay, *The International Regulation of Pharmaceutical Drugs*, American Society of International Law: Studies in Transnational Legal Policy No. 14 (Washington 1976); and D.C. Jayasuriya, *Regulation of Pharmaceuticals in Developing Countries* (WHO, Geneva 1985), Annex 3. *See also* M. Schoepe, "International Regulation of Pharmaceuticals: a WHO International Code of Conduct for the Marketing of Pharmaceuticals," *Syracuse Journal of International Law and Commerce*, vol. 11 (1984) pp. 121–141.

147. Part of the OECD guidance documents in this field were subsequently transformed into regulatory requirements in the European Community. E.g., *see* EEC Council Directive 88/320 on the Inspection and Verification of Good Laboratory Practice (GLP) (*Official Journal of the European Communities*, No. L 145 of 11 June 1988), as amended by EEC Commission Directive 90/18 (*Official Journal of the European Communities*, No. L 11 of 13 January 1990).

148. *United Nations Treaty Series*, vol. 956 p. 3. *See also* the 1979 EFTA "scheme for the mutual recognition of evaluation reports on pharmaceutical products," a voluntary understanding to facilitate the registration of foreign pharmaceuticals (signed by Austria, Finland, Norway, Sweden and Switzerland).

149. 79/831/EEC (*Official Journal of the European Communities*, No. L 259), amending for the sixth time Directive 67/548/EEC (*Official Journal of the European Communities*, No. L 196 of 16 August 1967). *See* R.A. Wyman Jr., "Control of Toxic Substances: The Attempt to Harmonize the Notification Requirements of the U.S. Toxic Substances Control Act and the European Community Sixth Amendment," *Virginia Journal of International Law*, vol. 20 (1980) pp. 417–458. For a list of other relevant EEC Directives (on agricultural chemicals, food additives and contaminants, consumer products, etc.) *see Health Aspects of Chemical Safety: Legislative and Administrative Procedures for the Control of Chemicals*, (World Health Organization Regional Office for Europe, Copenhagen 1984), annex II, pp. 243–254; and S.P. Johnson &

G. Corcelle, *The Environmental Policy of the European Communities* (London 1989).

150. Leive (note 107 above, vol. II p. 575) points out that article 22 of the WHO international health regulations, which actually provides for international certification upon request, was never applied and that national certification continues to be more acceptable in practice (p. 592).

151. Note 25 above.

152. Leive (note 107 above) vol. II p. 574.

153. *United Nations Treaty Series*, vol. 335 p. 211, as amended and supplemented by technical regulations through 1990. E.g., *see* Regulation No. 15 ("uniform provisions concerning the approval of vehicles equipped with a positive-ignition engine or with a compression-ignition engine with regard to the emission of gaseous pollutants by the engine"); *United Nations Treaty Series*, vol. 740 p. 364 (to be replaced in 1990 by consolidated Regulation No. 83). On the relationship with concurrent EEC regulations in this field, *see* P. Roqueplo, *Pluies acides: menaces pour l'Europe* (Paris 1988) pp. 297–307.

154. Article 1(5) of the 1958 Agreement provides that after deposit with the U.N. Secretariat by at least two Contracting Parties and subsequent communication by the U.N. to all parties, a new or amended text "shall enter into force as a Regulation annexed to this Agreement for all Contracting Parties which have informed the Secretary-General of their acceptance of it within three months from the date of the Secretary-General's communication."

155. Canada, Japan and the United States participate regularly in the UN/ECE Working Party on the Construction of Vehicles (WP29), which is in charge of drafting the technical regulations and amendments to the 1958 Agreement. Australia also keeps liaison with the Working Party and reports on national regulations aligned on the ECE rules. *See* the comments by Japan and the United States, "International Harmonization of Motor Vehicle Regulation," U.N. Docs. TRANS/SC1/WP29/R.454 and Add.1 (1987).

156. *See* the reports by Austria, Norway, Sweden and Switzerland, in: *The State of Transboundary Air Pollution* (note 63 above) pp. 9–10. In a *Declaration on Air Pollution by Motor Vehicles*, signed at Stockholm on 5 July 1985, the environment ministers of Austria, Canada, Denmark, Finland, Liechtenstein, Norway, Sweden and Switzerland agreed to cooperate towards the introduction of national engine emission standards following 1983 U.S. federal standards. The "Stockholm Group" has since continued to meet informally at the technical level (with the additional participation of the Federal Republic of Germany and the Netherlands), and played a significant role in the negotiation of tighter standards under the 1958 Agreement in the ECE Inland Transport Committee. *See* P.H. Sand, "Air Pollution in Europe: International Policy Responses," *Environment*, vol. 29 No. 10 (1987) pp. 16–29, at p. 19.

157. A.J. Toynbee, *A Study of History: Reconsiderations*, vol. 12 (Oxford 1961), p. 343: i.e., "the reception and adoption of elements of culture that have been created elsewhere and have reached the recipient by a process of diffusion."

158. *See* E.N. Rogers, *Diffusion of Innovations* (New York 1962); and T. Hagerstrand, Innovation Diffusion as a Spatial Process (Chicago 1967).

159. P.R. Gould, *Spatial Diffusion*, Association of American Geographers: Resource Paper No. 4 (Washington 1969) pp. 55–58.

160. *Faust*, Part I, Scene IV; Bayard Taylor's translation of 1870 (Oxford 1932).

161. Public Law 91–190, 83 Stat. 852 (1970). For a recent critical review of the Act by its principal draftsman, *see* L.C. Caldwell, "A Constitutional Law for the Environment: 20 Years with NEPA Indicates the Need," *Environment*, vol. 31 No. 10 (1989) pp. 6–11, 25–28.

162. *See* U.S. Senate Resolution No. 49 of 21 July 1978 ("International Environmental Assessment"); W.H. Mansfield, "Shaping Environmental Assessment for Use in International Activities," in: *Environmental Impact Assessment: Proceedings of a Seminar of the United Nations Economic Commission for Europe* (Oxford 1981) pp. 319–326. *See also* L.F.E. Goldie, "A General View of International Environmental Law: A Survey of Capabilities, Trends and Limits," in: *The Protection of the Environment and International Law* (A.C. Kiss ed., Alphen/Netherlands 1974) pp. 25–144, at pp. 124–140.

163. Goals and Principles of Environmental Impact Assessment, UNEP Governing Council Decision 14/25 of 17 June 1987, in U.N. Doc. UNEP/GC.14/17, annex III; "supported" by U.N. General Assembly Resolution 42/184 of 11 December 1987, paragraph 140. *See* J.E. Bonine, "Environmental Impact Assessment: Principles Developed," *Environmental Policy and Law*, vol. 17 (1987) pp. 5–9. The UNEP secretariat did, however, promote the use of EIA in multilateral development funding, in regional seas agreements (note 44 above), and generally in developing countries. *See* J. Mayda, *Manual on Environmental Legislation* (UNEP/IALS, Nairobi 1979); Y.J. Ahmad & G.K. Sammy, *Guidelines to Environmental Impact Assessment in Developing Countries* (London 1985); and UNEP Regional Office for Asia and the Pacific, *Environmental Impact Assessment: Basic Procedures for Developing Countries* (Bangkok 1988).

164. Australia enacted its Environment Protection (Impact of Proposals) Act on 17

December 1974 (No. 164, as amended by Act No. 12 of 3 April 1987); Zambia amended its 1970 Natural Resources Conservation Act (No. 53, *Zambia Government Gazette* Suppl.No. 123 p. 673) in 1981 to introduce impact assessments for major water development projects.

165. Articles 27 and 28, Decree No. 2811 of 18 December 1974, *Diario Oficial* vol. 111 No. 34243 (1975). *See* G.J. Cano, "Comprehensive Environmental Legislation: A Summary Review of Colombia's Environmental Code," *Environmental Policy and Law*, vol. 1 (1976) p. 177–179.

166. Royal Decree No. 1302 of 28 June 1986, *Boletín Oficial* No. 155 (30 June 1986) p. 2373; English translation by FAO, *Food and Agricultural Legislation*, vol. 36 No. 2 (1987) p. 173.

167. Act No. 76–629 of 10 July 1976, *Journal Officiel* No. 162 (13 July 1976) p. 4203; implemented by Decree No. 77–1141 of 12 October 1977.

168. Article 130, Act No. 83–03 of 5 February 1983, *Journal Officiel* No. 6 (8 February 1983) p. 250; English translation by WHO, *International Digest of Health Legislation*, vol. 35 (1984) p. 176.

169. Federal Act on Environmental Impact Assessment (UVPG) of 12 February 1990, *Bundesgesetzblatt I* (1990) p. 205; *see* P.C. Storm, "Environmental Impact Assessment in the Legal System of the Federal Republic of Germany," *University of Puerto Rico Law Review* (forthcoming, 1990).

170. Council Directive 85/337/EEC of 27 June 1985 on the Assessment of the Effects of Certain Public and Private Projects on the Environment, *Official Journal of the European Communities*, No. L 175 (5 July 1985) p. 40; *see* M. Grant, "Implementation of the European Community Directive on Environmental Impact Assessment,"

Connecticut Journal of International Law, vol. 4 (1989) pp. 463–477.

171. Article 4(3), Investment Decree of 30 November 1988, *Gesetzblatt*, Pt.I No. 26 (16 December 1988) p. 289. On earlier environmental controls in GDR regional investment planning, *see* P.H. Sand, "The Socialist Response: Environmental Protection Law in the German Democratic Republic," *Ecology Law Quarterly*, vol. 3 (1973) pp. 451–505, at pp. 470–471.

172. *See* A.O. Hirschman, *Development Projects Observed* (Washington 1967) pp. 21–28, referring to the fashion of presenting new river valley development schemes (in Brazil, Mexico, Colombia, Iran and India) as true copies of the Tennessee Valley Authority ("pseudo-imitation"). *See also* R.P. Dore, "The Prestige Factor in International Affairs," *International Affairs*, vol. 51 (1975) pp. 190–207.

173. *See* A.V. Kneese & B.T. Bower, *Managing Water Quality: Economics, Technology, Institutions* (Baltimore 1968) pp. 237–253, 257–262; and R.W. Johnson & G.M. Brown, *Cleaning Up Europe's Waters: Economics, Management and Policies* (New York 1976).

174. *See* P.H. Sand, "Pollution Sanctions: New Alternatives to Civil Liability," *Journal of Business Law*, (April 1973) pp. 147–154; and *Environmental Improvement Through Economic Incentives* (F.R. Anderson ed., Baltimore 1977).

175. For a survey of current national practice in OECD member countries, *see* J.B. Opschoor & H.B. Vos, *Economic Instruments for Environmental Protection* (OECD, Paris 1989); *see also* J.C. Bongaerts & R.A. Kraemer, "Permits and Effluent Charges in the Water Pollution Control Policies of France, West Germany and the Netherlands," *Environmental Monitoring and Assessment*, vol. 12 (1989) pp. 127–147.

176. *See* J. Salzwedel, *Studien zur Erhebung von Abwassergebühren* [Studies on Effluent Charges for Waste Water] (Berlin 1972) pp. 23–33; and P.H. Sand, "Environmental and Water Law in East Germany: National and International Aspects," in: *Environmental Law: International and Comparative Aspects* (J. Nowak ed., London 1976) pp. 77–84.

177. For the U.S., *see* Kneese & Bower (note 173 above) pp. 143–164, 315–318; and *Effluent Charges on Air and Water Pollution*, Environmental Law Institute Monograph Series No. 1 (E.I. Selig ed., Washington 1973). New USSR legislation on an environmental fund to be financed from emission charges is reported in UN/ECE, *The State of Transboundary Air Pollution* (note 63 above) p. 10.

178. *See* Opschoor & Vos (note 175 above) pp. 47–49; and *Pollution Charges in Practice* (OECD, Paris 1980) pp. 92–97.

179. Act on Environmental Tax for Domestic Air Traffic, of 15 December 1988, *Svensk Författnings-Samling* (1988) p. 1566.

180. *See* Sand (note 171 above) pp. 477–478; and article 18, Fifth Decree Implementing the National Environment Act (Air Quality Decree) of 12 February 1987, *Gesetzblatt* Pt.I No. 7 (27 March 1987).

181. *See* United Nations Economic Commission for Europe, *National Strategies and Policies for Air Pollution Abatement*, U.N. Doc. E.87.II.E.29 (1987) p. 16.

182. Decree No. 85–582 of 7 June 1985, Journal Officiel (9 June 1985) p. 6403.

183. Amendments of the fuel tax (pro-rated according to carbon content), the oil-spill protection charge and the waste-oil charge, adopted on 22 September 1989, are in force from 1 January to 31 December 1990. Together with other environmental taxes and

charges in the 1990 budget, they will amount to about 1 billion Finnish marks in revenues, representing slightly under one percent of the government's tax accrual. On the other hand, exemptions from turnover tax for environmental protection investments for this fiscal year will reduce state revenues by an estimated 400–500 million fin-marks; Ministry of the Environment, press release 89/uam3071/dt/ub/br/III (9 September 1989).

184. *Ekonomiska styrmedel i miljöpolitiken: energi och trafik* [Economic Instruments in Environmental Policy: Energy and Traffic], (Ministry of Environment and Energy, Stockholm 1989), English summary Pt.I, pp. 23–29; *see* E. Kessler, ''Sweden Proposes Charges on Emission of Pollutants to Finance Environmentally Sound Technology,'' *Ambio*, vol. 18 (1989) p. 462. For criticism of the proposal, *see International Environment Reporter*, vol. 13 No. 1 (10 January 1990) pp. 7–8.

185. *See* C. Seigneur, ''Economic Aspects of International Air Pollution Control Policies,'' *International Journal of Environmental Studies*, vol. 29 (1987) pp. 297–306, at pp. 298–299, for further references.

186. Opschoor & Vos (note 175 above) p. 36.

187. Umweltbundesamt [Federal Environmental Agency], *Information Sheet on the Environmental Label* (Berlin 1989); and J. Staupe, ''The German Environmental Label,'' unpublished paper prepared on behalf of the Federal Environmental Agency (30 August 1989).

188. The original ''Blue Angel'' was a vaudeville bar in a novel by Heinrich Mann, *Professor Unrat* (1905), title of a famous Marlene Dietrich movie by J. von Sternberg (1930).

189. Detailed environmental specifications for 60-odd eligible product groups are adopted and periodically updated by the jury; *see* RAL, *Umweltzeichen: Produktanforderungen* (Bonn 1989).

190. *See* the two most recent decisions rendered by the Federal Court of Justice, *VGU Cologne Fair Trade Association vs. Kaiser's Drugstore AG*, 20 October 1988, *Neue Juristische Wochenschrift*, vol. 42 (1989) pp. 711–714; and the critical review of earlier judgments by R. Wimmer, ''Ein Blauer Engel mit rechtlichen Macken,'' *Betriebs-Berater*, vol. 43 (1989) pp. 565–571.

191. 3273 products listed as of 31 December 1989, with an annual increment of 400 expected for 1990; *see* the information bulletin issued by the Federal Ministry of Environment, Nature Conservation and Radiation Protection, *Umwelt*, No. 2/1990, p. 62.

192. Under the ''Environmental Choice Program,'' an advisory board established pursuant to the 1988 Canadian Environmental Protection Act develops and updates environmental guidelines for selected product categories, which after public review are promulgated in the *Canada Gazette* and publicized in an *EcoLogo Environmental Choice Newsletter*. As of December 1989, 14 product category guidelines had been issued. Testing and certification of products is carried out under contract by the Canadian Standards Association, which then concludes licensing agreements (on an annual fee basis) with individual user companies.

193. Starting in February 1989, an EcoMark Secretariat established within the Japanese Environment Agency issues environmental criteria for selected commodities and concludes licensing contracts with users for two-year periods; *see Japan Environment Summary*, vol. 17 No. 3 (1989) pp. 1–2.

194. Nordic Council of Ministers, ''Guidelines for the Introduction of a Voluntary Nordic

Environmental Labelling Scheme,"
24.10.89/SP. Product selection criteria are to be laid down by a coordinating board (with one or two representatives from each member state) under the Council's Administrative Committee for Consumer Matters.

195. Some legal commentators refer to this practice as "public administration by the private sector"; U. Steiner, *Oeffentliche Verwaltung durch Private* (Hamburg 1975). The largest of the associations, TÜV Rhineland (Cologne), is increasingly involved in inspection contracts abroad.

196. The company's former ship division was restructured in 1988 as Det Norske Veritas Classification A.S. for a range of classification services internationally, including land-based wind turbines in Denmark and California; Det Norske Veritas, *Annual Report 1988* (Oslo 1989), pp. 11–18.

197. According to its *1988 Annual Report* (Geneva 1989), p. 4, SGS has been "involved as a privileged partner of the United Nations Environment Programme in the preparation of a draft convention dealing with the handling of toxic waste." The proximity of SGS headquarters was one of the points stressed by the Swiss Government in favour of locating the new UNEP secretariat for the Basel Convention (note 30 above) in Geneva.

198. *See* Staupe (note 187 above), p. 15, and the RAL product list (note 189 above).

199. *See* N. Schoon, "Germans Fill Green Gap in UK Market," *The Independent* (1 June 1989).

200. Wimmer (note 190 above), pp. 566–568, quoting the RAL guidelines for licence contracts.

201. National Research Council, *Toxicity Testing: Strategies to Determine Needs and Priorities* (Washington 1984).

202. Resolution 37/37 of 17 December 1982 on Protection against Products Harmful to Health and the Environment.

203. Section 17 of the 1964 Federal Insecticide, Fungicide and Rodenticide Act (FIFRA, as amended to 1978), and section 8 of the 1976 Toxic Substances Control Act (TSCA). *See* A. Gabbay, "International Ramifications of the Toxic Substances Control Act," *Harvard Environmental Law Review*, vol. 3 (1979) pp. 136–159; and K.A. Goldberg, "Efforts to Prevent Misuse of Pesticides Exported to Developing Countries: Progressing Beyond Regulation and Notification," *Ecology Law Quarterly*, vol. 12 (1985) pp. 1025–1051.

204. *See* note 97 above.

205. UNEP Governing Council Decision 14/27 of 17 June 1987.

206. FAO Conference, 23rd Session, Resolution 10/85, FAO Doc. C85/REP; *see* article 9 (Information Exchange), *International Code of Conduct on the Distribution and Use of Pesticides* (FAO, Rome 1986).

207. *See also* the European Community's Council Regulation 88/1734 of 16 June 1988 on EEC Imports and Exports of Certain Dangerous Chemical Products, *Official Journal of the European Communities*, No. L 155 (22 June 1988).

208. *See* J. Huismans, "Towards a World Black List of Chemicals?," *IRPTC Bulletin*, vol. 6 Nos. 2–3 (1984) p. 2.

209. Note 25 above.

210. Thirteenth Annual Report of the Secretariat, CITES Doc. 7.7 (1989) p. 7. A French proposal to restrict unilateral appendix III listings to the biennial CITES Conferences was unsuccessful; Resolution 7.15 adopted at the 1989 Lausanne Conference merely "encourages" declarations

concerning appendix III to be made during conference meetings; *see Traffic Bulletin*, vol. 11 (1990) p. 25.

211. Notifications regarding national legislation ranked second in numbers among the 93 notifications to Parties issued by the CITES Secretariat between January 1988 and June 1989; Thirteenth Annual Report (note 210 above) p. 26.

212. The same is true for appendix III listings generally, which frequently provoke formal reservations by importing countries unwilling to accept the additional enforcement burden involved.

213. *See* D.M. Johnston, "Marine Pollution Agreements: Successes and Problems," in: *International Environmental Diplomacy* (J.E. Carroll ed., Cambridge 1988) pp. 199–206, at p. 204.

214. *See* J.G. Ruggie, "International Responses to Technology: Concepts and Trends," *International Organization*, vol. 29 (1975) pp. 557–583, at p. 570; P.M. Haas, "Ozone Alone, No CFCs: Epistemic Communities and the Protection of Stratospheric Ozone," *Millenium*, vol. 19 (forthcoming, 1990); and P.M. Haas, "Do Regimes Matter? Epistemic Communities and Mediterranean Pollution Control," *International Organization*, vol. 43 (1989) pp. 377–403.

215. Ruggie (note 214 above), borrowing a term from Michel Foucault, *The Order of Things* (transl. New York 1973).

216. Note 25 above.

217. Notes 146, 147, 204 and 205 above.

218. Note 30 above.

219. Note 153 above.

220. Note 56 above.

221. Note 83 above.

222. Ernst Haas (note 6 above) p. 368.

223. *See* S.C. McCaffrey, "The Work of the International Law Commission Relating to Transfrontier Environmental Harm," *New York University Journal of International Law and Politics*, vol. 20 (1988) pp. 715; and the progress reports by McCaffrey in *American Journal of International Law*, vol. 81 (1987) pp. 668–681, vol. 82 (1988) pp. 144–165, vol. 83 (1989) pp. 153–171 and 937–945.

224. The Trail Smelter Arbitration, *Reports of International Arbitral Awards*, vol. 3 (United Nations, New York 1949), p. 1905. *See* J.E. Read, "The Trail Smelter Dispute," *Canadian Yearbook of International Law*, vol. 1 (1963) pp. 213–229; and M.M. Whiteman, *Digest of International Law*, vol. 6 (U.S. State Department, Washington 1968) pp. 253–256.

225. Note 56 above; footnote 1 to article 8(f) of the convention reads: "The present Convention does not contain a rule on State liability as to damage."

226. *British South Africa Co. vs. Companhia de Moçambique*, (1893) Appeal Cases p. 602, as subsequently interpreted by Canadian courts; e.g., in *Albert vs. Fraser Cos. Ltd.*, Dominion Law Reports, vol. 1 (1937) p. 39.

227. *See* J. Willis, "Jurisdiction of Courts: Action to Recover Damages for Injury to Foreign Land," *Canadian Bar Review*, vol. 15 (1937) pp. 112–115. Although the Lords' *Moçambique* rule was arguably resurrected in a 1970 environmental case by the South African Supreme Court (in *South Atlantic Islands Development Corp. Ltd. vs. Buchan*, South African Law Reports 1971 pt. 1 p. 234C), it may be doubted whether Canadian courts would uphold the rule today.

228. Read (note 224 above) p. 223.

229. *W. Poro vs. Houillères du Bassin de Lorraine (HBL)*, judgment of 22 October 1957 by the

Court of Appeals (Oberlandesgericht) of Saarbrücken, *Neue Juristische Wochenschrift*, vol. 11 (1958) p. 752; for an English summary *see* P.H. Sand, "The Role of Domestic Procedures in Transnational Environmental Disputes," in: OECD, *Legal Aspects of Transfrontier Pollution* (H. van Edig ed., Paris 1977) pp. 146–202, at pp. 148–149.

230. *See* S.C. McCaffrey, *Private Remedies for Transfrontier Environmental Disturbances*, IUCN Environmental Policy and Law Paper No. 8 (Morges/Switzerland 1975); and T. Bunge, "Transboundary Cooperation between France and the Federal Republic of Germany," in: *Transboundary Air Pollution: International Legal Aspects of the Cooperation of States* (C. Flinterman, B. Kwiatkowska & J.G. Lammers eds., Dordrecht 1986) pp. 181–198.

231. *See* Lammers (note 35 above) pp. 451–456; and A.H. Darrell, "Killing the Rhine: Immoral, But Is It Illegal?," *Virginia Journal of International Law*, vol. 29 (1989) pp. 421–472.

232. *International Legal Materials*, vol. 8 (1969) p. 229, and vol. 28 (1989) p. 620.

233. *United Nations Treaty Series*, vol. 1092 p. 279.

234. For background *see* the proceedings of the Transatlantic Colloquy on Cross-Border Relations: European and North American Perspectives (S. Ercmann ed., Zurich 1987).

235. Texts in OECD, *Legal Aspects of Transfrontier Pollution* (note 229 above) pp. 11–34.

236. U.N.Doc. ENVWA/AC.3/R.5 (1989); *see* the report of the third session of the Senior Advisers to ECE Governments on Environmental and Water Problems, U.N.Doc. ECE/ENVWA/14, paragraphs 25–26 (1990).

237. *See* Leive (note 107 above) vol. II p. 584; A.L. Levin, *Protecting the Human Environment:*

Procedures and Principles for Preventing and Resolving International Controversies (UNITAR, New York 1977) pp. 31–38; R.B. Bilder, "The Settlement of Disputes in the Field of the International Law of the Environment," *Recueil des Cours: Collected Courses of the Hague Academy of International Law*, vol. 144 (1975–I) pp. 139–239, at p. 224; and R. Fisher, *Improving Compliance with International Law* (Charlottesville, VA 1981) pp. 214–222.

238. Note 17 above.

239. Draft Non-Compliance Procedure, as annexed to the report of the first meeting of the Ad Hoc Working Group of Legal Experts on Non-Compliance with the Montreal Protocol, U.N.Doc. UNEP/OzL.Pro.LG.1/3 (proposed as new Annex D to the Protocol); reprinted in *Environmental Policy and Law*, vol. 19 (1989) p. 223.

240. Paragraph 14 of the above-mentioned report. *See* the note on the first meeting, "Non-Compliance with Ozone Agreement," *Environmental Policy and Law*, vol. 19 (1989) pp. 147–148.

241. *United Nations Treaty Series*, vol. 298 p. 3.

242. *See* J. Mertens de Wilman & I.M. Verougstrate, "Proceedings against Member States for Failure to Fulfil Their Obligations," *Common Market Law Review*, vol. 7 (1970) pp. 385–406; and H.A.H. Audretsch, *Supervision in European Community Law* (Utrecht 1978).

243. *See* Scheuing (note 73 above) p. 192; and I. Pernice, "Kompetenzordnung und Handlungsbefugnisse der Europäischen Gemeinschaft auf dem Gebiet des Umwelt- und Technikrechts" [The European Community's system of competences and authority to act in the field of environmental and technological law], *Die Verwaltung*, vol. 22 (1989) pp. 1–54.

244. Sixth annual report to the European Parliament on Commission monitoring of the application of Community law—1988, *Official Journal of the European Communities*, No. C 330 (30 December 1989) pp. 1–160; *see* note 116 above. The previous (fifth) report appears in the *Official Journal*, No. C 310 (5 December 1988); *see* L. Kraemer, "Du controle de l'application des directives communautaires en matiere de l'environnement," *Revue du Marché Commun* (1988) pp. 22–40.

245. *See* Pernice (note 243 above) p. 40.

246. Commission of the European Communities, *Information Memo* P/90/5 (8 February 1990).

247. Directive 80/779 of 15 July 1980, *Official Journal of the European Communities*, No. L 229 (30 August 1980); *see* J. Smeets, "Air Quality Limits and Guide Values for Sulphur Dioxide and Suspended Particulates: A European Community Directive," *Environmental Monitoring and Assessment*, vol. 1 (1982) pp. 373–382.

248. N. Haigh, "Impact of the EEC Environmental Programme: The British Example," *Connecticut Journal of International Law*, vol. 4 (1989) pp. 453–462, at p. 458 n.11; *see also* N. Haigh, *EEC Environmental Policy and Britain* (2nd rev.ed., London 1989).

249. Court of Justice of the European Communities, Joined cases 227/85 to 230/85, Reports of Cases before the Court (1988–1) pp. 1–12; summary in *Official Journal of the European Communities*, No. C 37 (9 February 1988) p. 4.

250. *The Financial Times* of 7 April 1989, p. 2; *see* Sands (note 129 above) p. 415 n.98. The proceedings in this case were triggered by a complaint from a non-governmental organization (Friends of the Earth).

251. *See* Pernice (note 243 above) and Kraemer (note 244 above). In the light of this new trend, some already see the role of the EEC Commission as that of a "European environmental ombudsman" (Scheuing, note 73 above, p. 192).

252. For a summary of ILO conventions and recommendations on the working environment, *see Environmental Law: An In-Depth Review*, UNEP Report No. 2 (Nairobi 1981) pp. 53–64.

253. V.Y. Ghebali, *The International Labour Organization: A Case Study on the Evolution of U.N. Specialized Agencies* (Dordrecht 1989); *see also* A. Alcock, *History of the International Labour Organization* (London 1971).

254. E.A. Landy, *The Effectiveness of International Supervision: Thirty Years of I.L.O. Experience* (London 1966); *see also* N. Valticos, "Contrôle," in: *A Handbook on International Organizations* (R.J. Dupuy ed., Dordrecht 1988) pp. 332–353, at pp. 340–344.

255. *See* M. Bossyut, "The Development of Special Procedures of the UN Commission for Human Rights," *Human Rights Law Journal*, vol. 6 (1985) pp. 179–210; T. Meron, *Human Rights Law-Making in the United Nations: A Critique of Instruments and Process* (Oxford 1986); and A. Williams, "The United Nations and Human Rights," in: *International Institutions at Work* (P. Taylor & A.J.R. Groom eds., London 1988) pp. 114–129.

256. Note 25 above.

257. Note 56 above.

258. The first major (four-years) review was published in 1987 (note 181 above); the 1988 annual review was published in the UN/ECE *Air Pollution Studies* series, No. 5 (note 63 above).

259. *See* S. Brown & L.L. Fabian, "Toward Mutual Accountability in the Nonterrestrial

Realms," *International Organization*, vol. 29 (1975) pp. 877–892.

260. E.g., *see* the extensive parliamentary questions (by the "Greens") on CITES implementation in the Federal Republic of Germany, in preparation of the seventh Conference of the Parties; *Umwelt* No. 11 (1989) pp. 524–532. *See also* the conclusions by Leive (note 107 above) vol. II p. 576, on the importance of publicizing non-compliance ("mobilization of shame to induce compliance"); and similar comments by G. Handl & R. Lutz, "An International Policy Perspective on the Trade of Hazardous Materials and Technologies," *Harvard International Law Journal*, vol. 30 (1989) pp. 351–374, at p. 373.

261. Local environmental audits have been organized by FoE at the county level in the United Kingdom since 1988.

262. *See* the UNEP survey of environmental auditing practices in *Industry and Environment*, vol. 11 No. 4 (1988) pp. 3–21; J. Palmisano, "Environmental Auditing: Past, Present and Future," *Environmental Auditor*, vol. 1 (1989) pp. 7–20; and The Environmental Audit: A Green Filter for Company Policies, Plants, Processes and Products (WWF/UK, Godalming 1989).

263. 56th session of the ICC Executive Board (Paris, 29 November 1988); text in *Environmental Policy and Law*, vol. 19 (1989) pp. 82–84.

264. Statement to the World Federation of United Nations Associations (WFUNA), Halifax, 5 June 1988; M. Strong, "The United Nations in an Interdependent World," *International Affairs* (Moscow), No. 1 (1989) pp. 11–21, at p. 20. *See also* T.M. Franck, "Soviet Initiatives: U.S. Responses—New Opportunities for Reviving the United Nations System," *American Journal of International Law*, vol. 83 (1989) pp. 531–544, at p. 541.

265. *See* P.S. Thacher, "International Mechanisms and Global Changes," *Environmental Conservation*, vol. 14 (1987) pp. 191–193.

266. Haas (note 6 above) p. 389.

267. The Centre has succeeded in mobilizing world-wide support for the Brundtland Report's concept of "sustainable development" among intergovernmental and non-governmental organizations, especially through a network of more than 120 "working partners" from all sectors; *see* the regular reports on follow-up activities in the *Brundtland Bulletin* (No. 6, December 1989).

268. Note 17 above, article 6.

269. Note 31 above; and Report of the first session of the third meeting of the Open-ended Working Group of the Parties to the Montreal Protocol, U.N. Doc. UNEP/OzL.Pro.WG.III(1)/3 (1990). *See* J. Koehler & S.A. Hajost, "The Montreal Protocol: A Dynamic Agreement for Protecting the Ozone Layer," *Ambio*, vol. 19 (1990) pp. 82–86.

270. Note 32 above, articles 2(3) and 5.

271. Note 30 above, article 15(7).

272. U.N. General Assembly Resolution 44/228 of 22 December 1989.

273. The present analysis draws on an unpublished study of "revision clauses" in environmental agreements, prepared for the German Federal Parliament's Commission of Enquiry on Protection of the Atmosphere, by Dr. Lothar Gündling, Max Planck Institute for Comparative Public Law and International Law (Heidelberg 1989).

274. J.T. Mathews, "Redefining Security," *Foreign Affairs*, vol. 68 (1989) pp. 162–177, at p. 176.

World Resources Institute

1709 New York Avenue, N.W.
Washington, D.C. 20006, U.S.A.

The World Resources Institute (WRI) is a policy research center created in late 1982 to help governments, international organizations, and private business address a fundamental question: How can societies meet basic human needs and nurture economic growth without undermining the natural resources and environmental integrity on which life, economic vitality, and international security depend?

Two dominant concerns influence WRI's choice of projects and other activities:

The destructive effects of poor resource management on economic development and the alleviation of poverty in developing countries; and

The new generation of globally important environmental and resource problems that threaten the economic and environmental interests of the United States and other industrial countries and that have not been addressed with authority in their laws.

The Institute's current areas of policy research include tropical forests, biological diversity, sustainable agriculture, energy, climate change, atmospheric pollution, economic incentives for sustainable development, and resource and environmental information.

WRI's research is aimed at providing accurate information about global resources and population, identifying emerging issues, and developing politically and economically workable proposals.

In developing countries, WRI provides field services and technical program support for governments and non-governmental organizations trying to manage natural resources sustainably.

WRI's work is carried out by an interdisciplinary staff of scientists and experts augmented by a network of formal advisors, collaborators, and cooperating institutions in 50 countries.

WRI is funded by private foundations, United Nations and governmental agencies, corporations, and concerned individuals.